CREATE A HOME YOU LOVE

Copyright © 2022 by Amy Taylor

Published by Wisteria Enterprises
wisteriaenterprises.com.au

All rights reserved. No part of this book may be reproduced in any manner whatsoever without written permission except in the case of brief quotations embodied in critical articles and reviews.

First Edition, 2022

Print Book ISBN: 9780648345633

CREATE A HOME YOU LOVE

AMY TAYLOR

Wisteria Enterprises

To Patrick,
without whose tantrum we would
never have created these ripples.

Contents

Dedication — iv

— 1

Step 1: Tear up your TODO List to take care of TODAY. — 3

T is for TADA — 6

O is for Options — 8

D is for Daily Intentions (#DailyFROG) — 11

A is for ACT — 15

Y is for versions of YOU!! — 18

Overview: 4 Dimensions of Success — 21

Part 1: Heart — 24

Step 2: The HEART of the matter — 25

Reconnecting with Hope — 27

Exploring Energy and Archetypes — 30

Uncovering Relationships and Thinking Patterns — 37

Step 3: Discover what the Experts Say	44
Decluttering	45
Organising	51
Maintaining	57
Part 2: Operations	62
Step 4 Make decisions in advance	63
Overcoming Decision Fatigue	65
Are they reasons or excuses?	70
Purpose Statement	75
Step 5 Using EASE and GRACE to make PLANS	81
Deciding with Ease	83
Getting organised with GRACE	88
A place for everything and everything in its place	92
Step 6 - Strategic Planning	99
5 types of Plans	102
Choosing your Household Categories	110
Making the invisible visible	114
Part 3: Movement	118
Step 7 Creating Sustainable Habits	120
Start with Easy Wins	121
Build on success	126

The Habit Management Matrix	132
Step 8 - Create a Sanctuary	138
Choose your Starting Point	140
Three styles of decluttering.	145
To sell or not to sell. That is the question.	150
Step 9 Getting your family on board	154
Apply the TODAY Principles to your family	156
Be Inspirational - take care of yourself first.	160
Take the pressure off you and your family, by finding a community	164
Part 4: Experiences	168
About Wisteria Enterprises	169
Acronym and Model List	171
Task Summary	173
About Amy Taylor	179

Dear Friends,

Who would have ever thought that the tantrum of a 4-year-old child could create such significant ripples? Certainly not me in the moment.

I'll share more about that turning point in chapter one, for now I want to address why I called you friends, when clearly some of you are strangers to me, and I to you...

Friends is not a term I use lightly; generally, I keep it fairly reserved. However, as you read through these pages, as I write them, I must keep in my mind that I am speaking to friends. These pages are filled with vulnerabilities, they are filled with tears, heartaches, and joy.

What I share between these pages are not everyday conversations that you would have with someone in the supermarket queue, they are heartfelt confessions I would only share with my friends.

Throughout these pages, designed to bring you a sense of peace and calm as you bring more focus to how you manage and organise your home, I will share openly and transparently my experiences, and so I call you friend.

You are probably here because you want to create a different experience for yourself in your home. And I will help you. But take note this is not about having a spotless house by the time you finish the book. Our houses didn't become cluttered or unclean in a season, it's a build-up over time, and it will take time to reclaim them.

This is about going on a journey and transforming your house into a home. A home that fills your heart with joy, that runs smoothly, and that empowers you to keep moving through life passionately.

Together, we will explore the thinking that created the chaos, some alternatives, and how to create the systems for you to manage your household.

This is not a sit back and read kind of book. Just opening the pages won't change your experience. If you only read and don't take action, you will not get success. Creating a home you love is a hands-on experience with actions to be taken.

The more you choose to engage with the words on the pages the more success you will feel, though I will say nothing beats being cheered on and championed by others. Share this with your friends, join the online community where you can connect with others on the journey.

Everyone starts at different levels and wherever you are is okay.

I look forward to sharing through this book and beyond as you create a sense of stability, start to feel more in control, and build the platform from which you will create a home where you feel calm and content.

Step 1: Tear up your TODO List to take care of TODAY.

While todo lists can feel like they are helping us, the mindset we bring around them can be a major productivity killer. Todo lists often create a sense of pressure, overwhelm, or obligation. And so today, we're going to dump them and many people at this point start to freak out. That's okay. If you're freaking out, that's okay. If you're rejoicing, thinking you're never going to have to look at a list again, it's not what's going to happen.

In this first section of the book, we are going to start by identifying three different types of lists we can use to replace our Todo lists and find a more fulfilling way to get shit done today.

One of the fastest ways to kill our motivation to take action, and therefore our productivity, is to only focus on what we have to do, never taking time to reflect on what is being done.

TODO lists can be the worst for this. We want to embrace

a mentality of progress not perfection. This is where TADA lists come in.

We want to make sure we are noticing progress. I've lost count now of the number of years since I started using these to boost my confidence, restore my self-esteem, and remind myself I am more capable than I sometimes remember.

It was a fairly standard day when my son, in full meltdown because I asked him to put his plate in the sink (the horror!!) screamed at me: "You never do anything" and his words pierced my heart.

You see, while I knew he was simply angry and didn't really mean what he said, I felt it to my core because on some level I felt like I didn't do enough. Like I wasn't enough. (Neither were true of course, but it's not always easy to remember that in the heat of the moment when you already feel worthless and run down).

At the time my husband and I had 3 children under 5, my post-natal depression was kicking back in, and it's highly possible I was pregnant with child number 4. Hormones, sleep deprivation, and constant challenges to my worth meant I took it very, very personally.

Not the first time. Before this day, (and some days since) in those moments of sheer heaviness falling on my shoulders I have been known to fall apart and stay stuck in depression.

I really don't know what was different on that day, or where I learned the idea of a TADA list from (maybe Flylady, but I've never seen her speak about it since), but it was a turning point.

Instead of being weighed down by feelings of unworthiness I decided to prove (more to myself than the 4-year-old) that I did in fact do many worthwhile things each and every day. The following morning, I got up and started keeping track of everything I did.

By 9am, - I'd also filled an entire scrapbooking page with a list and increased my recognition that I do in fact attend to many things (despite what the house often looks like) and I had reconnected with my worth - so I allowed myself to stop tracking everything.

But the lesson stuck, and any time I feel unworthy, I feel challenged about if I am good enough, I remind myself that I am using the power of a TADA list.

T is for TADA

TADA stands for Things Already Done and Accomplished. And they can include big things, but I encourage you on your first attempt to really focus on the little things. The smallest of steps, taken today, can help us build a much brighter tomorrow. Take a few minutes now and record what you've done this morning.

If I was to start my list today it would read something like:

Stacked dishwasher. Moved washing to the dryer. Culled some emails. Added posts into a Facebook group. Got kids to school. Wrote the script for this video. And so on.

Embrace that taking action on the little things can lead to the big things. And they are all worthy of acknowledging and celebration.

A todo list is indiscriminate, and it's long and it's endless and reminds us what we haven't done. A TADA list, also long and endless, reminds us of what we have done.

If this doesn't excite you or light you up or you have some fears of not knowing what you need to get done by throwing away your TODO list and replacing it with a TADA, keep reading. The Options list and DailyFROG principles are designed to address this.

However, I do invite you to pause reading right now, and write the TADA list. Use this list as often as you need to be reminded you are Awesome. That may be a few times a day to start. For me, generally, now it's once a week or so. There's no right or wrong. Just start with a list. Celebrate your Progress. Own your Success. In doing so we invite more of it into our lives.

TASK: *Complete a list with the heading: I choose to acknowledge these 5 TADA's (Things Already Done & Accomplished)*

O is for Options

Like our TODO and TADA lists, Options lists can also be long and endless. However, for most people the shift in name from Todo to Options is enough to remove some of the associated obligation, pressure and overwhelm many have with a todo list.

This section is all about us learning to recognise and embrace choice. One way we can do this is by renaming our lists from todo to Options.

Commonly when I share this philosophy people resist because they believe something like: "If everything on my list is an option then I won't take action". I understand this resistance and invite you for five days to embrace the possibility that even if you aren't pressured or obligated you will indeed take action.

I promise you the world won't fall apart if you don't get everything done. Chances are that if you are working from a space of obligation, pressure, or stress your Todo lists aren't all getting done anyway. I've seen many people with a Todo list that is never completed - and they feel miserable as a result.

Perhaps it's time to embrace Options. Embrace possibilities. Embrace the freedom of choice.

I want you to think about what it would mean for you if you recognised all your tasks are indeed choices, they are options, (we will talk about things that are required in the #DailyFROG section of the book), for now, embrace a sense of lightness.

If you are not yet a list person, I want you to consider what Matthew McConaughey says in the opening of his book Greenlights. It's something like: "I don't write things down to remember; I write them down to be able to forget." I really love this philosophy. By using lists we are able to clear our mind and bring focus to life. One of the keys to productivity is being able to focus on what matters most, which means being able to forget (because it is documented elsewhere) the things that aren't important.

TASK: *I invite you to take 10 minutes now and do what's often called a braindump, writing down as many Options as you can handle looking at, that are available to you today.*

And then pick only one thing at a time and focus on that (forgetting everything else) until it is complete, knowing that the rest of your options will be available for you to come back to at any time.

If you feel like things are too big for you to stay focused on for long enough to complete, I suggest you add some tiny bite sized things to your options list. (We will talk more about how to do this even more effectively when we get to the section on Big Fish, Little Fish). For now, the simple and quick hack is to ensure you can do it in two minutes - if you can't - pick something you can by making it smaller.

Use the Brainstorm Technique to get everything out of your mind and on paper so you can forget, freeing your mind to focus on getting things done.

D is for Daily Intentions (#DailyFROG)

At this point, hopefully, you've tried using options lists, and TADA lists and are getting a sense of if they are helpful for you or not. I suggest you keep these practices up as we continue forward - try them for at least a week or two before you pass judgement on them.

Years ago, I read a book by Brian Tracey called Eat That Frog. A simple concept - start each day by doing the most important tasks first. Which is great, when you know what they are, and have clear priorities.

Too often we default to only taking care of one of the keys to productivity and fulfillment. I needed to know what the key priorities were, and this is where DailyFROG was born.

These four key areas of life, simple as they sound, have a great impact on our lives. DailyFROG allows us to hone in and ensure we are focused on ALL four key areas to design a life we love, day by day.

The four key pillars are ForMe, Required, Outstanding, & GiveValue.

Too often we only look at what is required of us. This

results in our FROG becoming FOG. FOG stands for Frustrated, Overwhelmed, and Guilt-ridden.

When we embrace all four pillars, daily, we get FROG: we allow ourselves to become Fulfilled, Resilient, Organised, & Gratified.

Each of these categories is simple by nature. They are deliberately named in a way that makes it obvious what they encompass. While the names are simple, it's not always easy to remember that each is just as valid as the other.

ForMe - is anything that helps you feel good within and about yourself.

Required - anything that leads you to meeting commitments - these could be work commitments, client commitments, or other promises you have made to others or yourself. They could be tasks, activities, or lifestyle choices.

Outstanding - This is taking care of the important, but not urgent things. It's going above and beyond to the items that are less likely to be noticed. These could be overdue or extraordinary in nature.

Give Value - This is focused on connecting with and helping, supporting, and championing others.

For each of these categories, you want to start with between 1 and 3 small, implementable items.

For example:

ForMe: Tea and Yoga

Required: Appointments in my calendar and one task from a project, like creating copy for a landing page.

Outstanding: Review an old program and revamp to give even more value to students.

GiveValue: Share a blog post and answer questions in a Facebook group. Smile at someone at the shopping centre.

Once you have created your list - the key is to take action.

When I first started, I used to aim to have removed my chances of FOG before 9am, leaving me space to do what is Required throughout the day.

These days I am a little more fluid and aim to have at least one item completed to clear the FOG by 9am.

Choose the desired time frame that works best for you. As long as you are doing them before you go to bed each night, this is what matters. This is how you will not only create a home you love, but a life that leaves you feeling fulfilled.

I do believe Brian Tracy had a point - we often leave things weighing over us, and if we had to eat a frog, the best way to do it in a way that gives us the most room to feel fulfilled and productive is to get it done as early as possible.

A DailyFROG list can be done first thing in the morning, or last thing before bed (preparing for the next day).

This sets you up for success. Start where you are. Take care of one day at a time before you aim to take care of everything else.

If you want to be fulfilled in your life, dedicate time to doing one thing from each of the four lists.

Of course, just writing the Options list and the DailyFROG list is not enough to create a home or life we love. That requires us to ACT. We will explore motivation strategies and how we can be more inspired to ACT in the next chapter.

TASK: *I invite you to write your DailyFROG list and choose one thing to do from each category.*

If you would like extra support, share in the online community.

A is for ACT

One of the most common struggles I encounter when working with clients is lack of motivation. So often we know what we need to do, but we just aren't feeling inspired. This led me to study many different areas of productivity and motivation.

One of the models I came across in my travels, Self-Determination Theory, suggests there are three basic needs that influence our motivation. Autonomy, Competence, and Relatedness. These three needs are something I unpack on a regular basis with my VIP clients.

Generally speaking, for us to take action we need to know we are surrounded by people who will support and champion us on our journey. This is why joining and participating in the DailyFROG group matters so much, both for you to tap into and be inspired as well as give value in sharing your own journey. Just knowing we are not alone matters so much when it comes to productivity and fulfillment.

Beyond relatedness, we need to have a level of Autonomy and Competence. Autonomy is the sense we can choose. Competence is based on our capability to do a task. Next to that is TIME.

These adjusted pillars make up the acronym ACT.

We are more likely to feel motivated when we have:

Autonomy, Competence & Time

While we need to feel other people are on the same journey as us (even if they are just someone we know by reading their book) it is even more imperative that we make time for what matters most to us.

TASK Summary: *If you haven't already set a reminder to take the time daily to:*

- plan and take action on your DailyFROG,

- create your options list, and

- celebrate your TADA's each and every day.

Each day I suggest you think about what motivates you and dedicate time to these activities. Develop competency not only in the skill of cleaning your home, but also managing yourself. And most of all keep coming back to reminding yourself of the choices in your life - for this is what creates Autonomy.

Take a moment now and rank yourself on each of these characteristics of motivation.

Autonomy - How much choice do you feel you have in your day to day activities?
(If this is low, perhaps check out todos vs options again...)

Competence - How capable do you feel to manage your home? To delegate effectively? To get on top of the organisation and strategy of creating a home you love?
(If this is low - keep reading we cover this in part 2 of this book is all about - building competencies in household

management).

Time - what are you spending your time on?
Are you dedicating time to each of the Pillars of fulfillment in the DailyFROG acronym?
Is there something you need to dedicate more time to?

If this is low, keep reading as we will address how to navigate the journey from thinking you need to be someone else to embracing who you truly are in the next section.

Y is for versions of YOU!!

One of the most common struggles I encounter when working with clients is lack of motivation. So often we know what we need to do, but we just aren't feeling inspired. This led me to study many different areas of productivity and motivation.

One of the models I came across in my travels, Self-Determination Theory, suggests there are three basic needs that influence our motivation. Autonomy, Competence, and Relatedness. These three needs are something I unpack on a regular basis with my VIP clients.

Generally speaking, for us to take action we need to know we are surrounded by people who will support and champion us on our journey. This is why joining and participating in the DailyFROG group matters so much, both for you to tap into and be inspired as well as give value in sharing your own journey. Just knowing we are not alone matters so much when it comes to productivity and fulfillment.

Beyond relatedness, we need to have a level of Autonomy and Competence. Autonomy is the sense we can choose.

Competence is based on our capability to do a task. Next to that is TIME.

These adjusted pillars make up the acronym ACT.

We are more likely to feel motivated when we have:

Autonomy, Competence & Time

While we need to feel other people are on the same journey as us (even if they are just someone we know by reading their book) it is even more imperative that we make time for what matters most to us.

TASK Summary: *If you haven't already set a reminder to take the time daily to:*

- plan and take action on your DailyFROG,

- create your options list, and

- celebrate your TADA's each and every day.

Each day I suggest you think about what motivates you and dedicate time to these activities. Develop competency not only in the skill of cleaning your home, but also managing yourself. And most of all keep coming back to reminding yourself of the choices in your life - for this is what creates Autonomy.

Take a moment now and rank yourself on each of these characteristics of motivation.

Autonomy - How much choice do you feel you have in your day-to-day activities?
(If this is low, perhaps check out todos vs options again...)

Competence - How capable do you feel to manage your home? To delegate effectively? To get on top of the organisation and strategy of creating a home you love?

(If this is low - keep reading we cover this in part 2 of this book is all about - building competencies in household management).

Time - what are you spending your time on?
Are you dedicating time to each of the Pillars of fulfillment in the DailyFROG acronym?
Is there something you need to dedicate more time to?

If this is low, keep reading as we will address how to navigate the journey from thinking you need to be someone else to embracing who you truly are in the next section.

Overview: 4 Dimensions of Success

It doesn't matter whether we are transforming our surroundings, building a business, or connecting more deeply in a relationship, everything in our lives comes back to these four core pillars.

Heart, Operations, Movement & Experiences.

HEART - At the core of this section...

The key components we find in our Heart are Hope, Energy, Archetypes, Relationships, & Thinking.

The H.O.M.E acronym is a thinking model. Adapted from the critical alignment model by Sharon Pearson, world-renowned coach, trainer and business owner. Managing a household follows many of the same principles as managing a business.

Operations is what helps us to Get R.E.A.D.Y.

It includes our Routines, Expectations, Agendas, Daily Intentions, and Your Checklists.

We would never dream of operating a business without an operations manual, yet many of us attempt to manage our households with no awareness of the things we do consistently, the steps we take, or the chores we take care of automatically. The real benefit of having an operations manual is that you can more easily invite others (like husbands, older children, or additional helpers) to assist you. Instead of needing to explain, we can simply hand over the checklist. I used these a lot when setting up my Mother-in-law to manage my house when I am away.

Movement is where we take action.

Without action, nothing gets done. The focus of this book is more on mindset (Heart) and our systems (Operations), you will also need to take action to create movement towards your house becoming a HOME you love. Movement is how we bring our Operations to life.

Experiences are where we gather feedback, discover how aligned our goals are with our Heart, and assess if we are feeling fulfilled yet.

Here we explore how we felt, what Movement we made (or didn't), and how we respond in different moments. I highly encourage you to share this element in our community. It will give you a chance to be championed, supported, validated and feel seen. Our hearts are healed and reconnected through relationships.

Over the next few chapters, we will dive more into the Heart component. We will then start to look at the key pieces of Operations and then some fast-tracked movements.

Of course, every chapter contains a little of each of the 4 dimensions. Your experience will help you discern your Heart. The movement you take will help you find the operations that are a good fit for you. Sometimes you may want to stretch yourself so you can create a new experience, this may mean taking action when you don't feel like it or changing a thinking pattern. Of course, you are in control, you can choose what works for you. Take what is helpful and speaks to your heart and leave the rest.

This is not about me telling you what to do, it's about a set of Options being offered up and allowing you to choose how you take it out and create a new experience and a home you love for yourself.

Part 1: Heart

Our Heart shapes our mindset, is the core of our drivers, and impacts our motivations, willingness, and desires and therefore influences our actions. Many of our drivers are unconscious, and so we will use the heart-centred content to get to know ourselves a little better, uncovering the hidden forces that influence how we act, deepening our self-awareness.

Step 2: The HEART of the matter

In this chapter we're going to look at our ideal outcome through the lens of our HEART. Like most things in my teaching and mentoring, HEART is an acronym.

Hope, Energy, Archetypes, Relationships & Thinking.

These five components create a target, a guideline of what we want in our lives. Without a clear target, we don't know where to aim, we can't assess if we are on track, and we don't know the path we need to take.

Of course, it's possible to get places without knowing the destination, but to quote the Cheshire Cat - if you don't know where you are headed then any path will do.

Whether you know it or not you already have a destination in focus. The question is: is what you have in your mind what you want or what you don't?

When we set out on an adventure, we can look through three perspectives. They are

1. What we are leaving behind, what we are moving away from, and what we don't want.

2. The obstacles, challenges, or roadblocks.
3. The new possibilities we seek, what we are moving towards, and what we do want.

If we continue to focus on what we don't want, we may not see the obstacles we need to overcome, and we are very rarely going to see the new possibilities.

If we stare at the obstacles, we won't see past them to the possibilities.

If we only focus on what we want, ignoring what we need to overcome and let go, we stay stuck in a perpetual loop of wishing, waiting, and hoping.

When we can look at what we're leaving behind, the obstacles we'll overcome, and the possibilities we are moving towards we create for ourselves a solid plan.

Over the next few chapters, aim to keep this in mind as you look to your heart for guidance to set what the end in mind looks like for you.

Reconnecting with Hope

The first piece of the heart we're going to explore is that of Hope.

Hope can be seen in two flavours. Passive and Active.

Passive Hope is when we wish and/or wait for the outcome to arrive without taking any action. I hope this works out. It's a level of optimism that is childlike in nature.

A sense of magical or wishful thinking. If I make a wish, my dreams will come true. It's behind sayings like dream-believe-achieve - which is missing a key step - action.

Active Hope has us hold onto the possibilities, keep an open mind, acknowledging any fears or doubts that may arise, and taking action anyway. Active hope moves us towards our dream, overcomes obstacles, and achieves success.

Active hope can be a replacement for self-belief. A few years ago, I decided to challenge myself by performing stand-up comedy live on stage. I had little to no belief in my ability that I could pull it off. My lifetime conditioning of not being funny was much stronger than anything else I could hold onto. The scales of evidence I could see were completely tipped in favour of my conditioning. I had no self-trust; with no reference points, how could I trust myself? My fear and doubts were massive - and cruel - suggesting in moments that I should bail in weird and wonderful ways.

But, despite all that, I had hope. An active Hope. I didn't have skills or talents in that area, so I set out to learn. I enrolled in comedy school, the training ran over five evenings culminating in my live performance to a paying audience.

I wanted to quit, but I knew if I followed the formulas they taught, I might succeed. I had hope. But I didn't just sit around wishing and waiting for success. I practised. I created post-it-note plans. I learned 12 minutes of content so I could forget half and still get through 5 minutes.

I didn't blindly Hope, I wasn't passive in my approach, I was exceptionally active. Despite the fact it felt so uncomfortable. I spent more time on the phone with my accountability buddy that week than any other week before or since.

I was literally dry retching in the bathroom 2 minutes before I walked on stage. Where my worst nightmare came true - I told a joke and no one laughed. Still, in that, the darkest of moments, literally, with the spotlight on me, I was looking into a dark abyss and couldn't see the audience, in that moment my active Hope kicked in. Keep talking, it said. I did what I'd practised. I self-deprecated. I made fun of the flopped joke. My hope was transformed into action.

If you are procrastinating, if you are consumed by fear and doubt into inaction, it's possible you are without hope, or stuck in passive Hope.

Turn this around today. Active Hope does things without knowing it will work out but holding onto faith that it will.

Active Hope believes that when we are the example others will follow our lead. Active Hope trusts that we can make choices about what to keep and what to let go and handle it if we toss or donate something significant.

Active Hope trusts that 5 minutes of action can make a difference.

TASK: *Active Hope puts a bookmark in the book and goes and does the dishes, or moves the washing from the machine into the dryer, or finds 10 pieces of rubbish to throw away. Active Hope Moves. Then comes back to read the next chapter.*

Exploring Energy and Archetypes

Contained within our Heart is the essence of our Energy and our Archetypes. Energy is reflective of our physical and psychological well-being. Archetypes are reflective of our soul's progress on the journey of life.

Both play a key part in how aligned we feel. How much we want to do things we love and are passionate about, or how much we avoid life in general. When our soul, psychological, and physical wellbeing are at their peak we are inspired and able to take action. When they are at a low point, we feel flat and unmotivated.

Each of these topics is a giant rabbit-hole that we are only briefly going to touch on in this book.

Physical energy is influenced by rest, nutrition, and overall health. This isn't an area I'm equipped to educate on beyond - rest well, eat well, and seek appropriate care for physical ailments or conditions.

Where I am more equipped to share insights and useful knowledge is in the area of Psychological Energy. There is so much I could share here.

So many psychological patterns that are in my realm of awareness. Right now, the one that seems most pressing and useful as you aim to create a home you love is that of the difference between a task, a title, and a transformation.

Caroline Myss, author of Sacred Contracts, talks about there being three levels of awareness. The literal, the interactive, and the archetypical. Professor Amy Wrzesniewski's research explores the experience of work as a job, career, or calling.

My own interpretation of the combination of these two models is that we can approach everything we are doing as a Task, a Title, or a Transformation.

A job is literal and focuses on the Tasks. We look at the dishes and we think about the task of washing the dishes. It doesn't fuel our soul, it's simply something we could tick off on our todo lists (if we still used them) or add to our Tada list.

A Career is interactive and focuses on living up to the Title, the slightly larger picture. We look at the dishes and know that our role in life is to manage the house. We take on the title of Mum, or Wife, or Household Manager and doing the dishes helps us fulfill this role. This includes making dirty things clean, and so we do the dishes, not as just a task, but part of the larger role we play at home, contributing to us owning our desired titles.

Or we can see the world (and our homes) as a playground for our transformations. To engage in a story, to look upon housework as a Calling, to access new awareness of ourselves and create transformative possibilities.

How we respond to the dishes could be through any of

these lenses. The more we are trapped in tasks the lower our energy will be. If all we do is live up to our titles, we lose sight of the bigger picture. The more we embrace the transformative possibilities in everything we do - the more we will feel energetically aligned and rejuvenated.

Everything in our lives can be seen through the archetypical level with transformative potential.

Do we see those reasons and feel the potential?

Are we open to the transformation or are we stuck in ticking off tasks?

Caroline Myss, in her book Sacred Contracts, suggests we have a contract with everything in our lives. Every person, every item, every action, everything we encounter all of these may be linked to our sacred contracts.

When we bring something into our home we deepen the possibilities in which we have a contract, big or small, with this item.

Dawn, from "The Minimal Mom", talks about the silent todo list, which to me is another version of the sacred contracts. We buy things to serve a purpose, but if we don't allow them to fulfil their purpose, we are letting down our side of the contract. This drains us of energy.

No one sets out to buy clutter, to fill their house with so much stuff that they can't breathe and end up consumed by the weight of all they own, and yet, so many of us are. We tell ourselves we need it, it's a bargain, we justify it through our identity, that it doesn't take up much space, that it might be useful one day, and yet, the moment it enters our house we take on an obligation, we form a contract to care for and use or enjoy said item.

When we declutter, we are letting go, dissolving the contractual obligations we created. We are no longer tied psychically to the item. While we hold onto the items, we allow it to keep a psychological hold over us. The core four archetypes, the survival archetypes, are generally the drivers of this.

While there are limitless archetypes, and many you will resonate with, every one of us has the core 4. These are our protectors and the parts of us that helped us survive life so far, so they are all I will speak to here. The core 4 survival archetypes are: The child, the prostitute, the saboteur, and the victim.

Each of these can play a part in our transition from household slave to household manager.

The child not wanting to take responsibility, the saboteur wanting to avoid the truth, the prostitute sacrificing spiritual fulfillment for material gains, and the victim playing the woe is me and its all too hard card.

Taking a leadership role is hard because we need to navigate our core companions, the ones that have helped us survive so long, and who we rely on in so many ways, and often they have possessed us and taken control of us.

The child collects things for the magic they hold, but they need guidelines and rules. The victim wants to blame someone else, but the truth is we did this, and we can step in, take back our power, and make our own choice. The prostitute falls into scarcity and is gathering to protect, if we have enough stuff we can survive, and yet we sell our soul to give up the space to the things, no more, we can identify our values, we can protect our soul and not give into the material world claims. The saboteur, the saboteur is subtle and sneaky, hidden in the justifications, the excuses. The saboteur is designed to test us to see if we truly know what matters, to see what warrants us taking a stand. And a house that is transformed from chaos to calm, from life-sucking to a sanctuary is worth it. We can reclaim control. We can take charge of our homes. We can create a life we love.

Navigating our survival archetypes and how they influence what we hold onto in our homes is simple enough, though not always easy.

Each of our survival archetypes is on a journey.

The child transitioning from reliant to managing responsibilities. (It would have got some insights from our early focus on taking care of Today).

The prostitute teaching us how to navigate the dance between physical survival instincts and living our values. (We will uncover more about her when we create our purpose statements in Chapter 4).

The victim discovers how to set clear boundaries and balance power dynamics to not be either victim or victor but to work in partnership with others. (This is addressed when we explore how to bring others on the journey in chapter 9).

The saboteur who helps us see our greatest fear is that of being self-empowered. Who seeks truth and can either be our greatest champion or our greatest critic. (Challenged and leveraged when we start to assess are we making excuses or choices in Chapter 4).

There is so much I could share on this, enough to fill a 10-week course easily. In fact, I have.

For now, notice which survival archetype seems to be

ruling your home. Read the four statements below and notice which statements you resonate with most.

Victim/Warrior
I need my home to protect me. Vs. I protect my home at all costs.

Prostitute/Lover
I do things I don't like to make my home feel safe. Vs. I Love being able to demonstrate care of my home.

Child/Sovereign
I want someone else to take care of my home. Vs. I rule over my home and make sure things that matter are taken care of.

Saboteur/ Magician
I just can't seem to maintain cleaning and tidying my home Vs. I create a Home I love.

Our archetypes play a huge influence in our lives, influencing our relationships and our thinking. Different archetypes will approach things differently. Tapping into your child you may be able to bring a more playful approach, accessing your Magician will bring more magic into your home.

As you go through the following sections on relationships and thinking you may notice that you have conflicting thoughts, this is simply two or more of your archetypes coming to life and sharing different perspectives.

TASK: *Start to explore which archetypes come out in different areas of your life and the energy they bring out in you.*

The relationship you have with the different parts of yourself will influence your ability to embrace life. This is taking what we learned about our versions of selves in the Y is for Versions of YOU section even deeper.

This journey can be much more in-depth than I am sharing in this book – it is enough for another book or course.

If you want to connect with more of your archetypes and build a team of champions, inside and out, please check out the resources available at: wisteiriaenterprises.com.au/resources

Uncovering Relationships and Thinking Patterns

Relationships are something that can happen with many things. The top 5 that impact our ability to create a home we love are:
- our past
- our passions
- our possessions
- people &
- perceptions

Our relationships, and the pathway they lead us down, are very closely linked to the beliefs we struggle to release.

If someone has a belief that housework is boring, based on past experiences that they found monotonous, and mundane they'll have a very different relationship with it than the person who believes housework is an opportunity for meditation, self-awareness, and the foundation of how we show up in the world playing out in how we manage our day-by-day tasks.

The person who believes leadership is about making people do things vs leadership is about empowering and expanding people's potential is going to approach bringing their family on board on this journey very differently.

We need to ask ourselves if the relationships we have with the past, our passions, the people we live with, our own perceptions, and our possessions, are those relationships creating a set of beliefs that serve and support you?

I don't believe in universal limiting beliefs; every belief has a place. With each belief there is a game played out based on that assumption. Each belief shapes the relationship we create.

When we play a board game, we understand the rules are there to help us to achieve the outcome.

The same is true of our beliefs. They shape how we move through the game of life, they direct our relationship with movement on the board.

What we are willing to do is shaped largely by our beliefs. Our relationship with housework, cleaning, clutter, delegating and so much more will shape how we move forward.

Some of your relationships will support you. Many are what create the chaos you are ready to leave behind.

Project yourself forward to a place where you have the house you dream of, where you are taking responsibility, championing yourself day by day, and living in harmony between physical and physiological desires.

What relationships does this version of you embody?

How do you relate with the past?
How do you engage with your passions?
How strong are the bonds with your possessions?
What do you value about the people in your life?
And how open are you when it comes to exploring and challenging your perceptions?

Many of the relationships we have, fuelling various beliefs, that got us here, that created this experience, will not be the ones that get us a different experience.

Someone who hates housework may need to change their relationship, via their beliefs, to embrace being a household manager.

There are so many different models we can use to explore our beliefs, but this book is not solely dedicated to that topic (at some point I may write a book on that alone).

The model I trust will add the most value to you creating a home you love is the 7 GIVENS. This framework is inspired by a model taught to me by my mentor, Joe Pane, in my advanced coaching training. It explores how our beliefs can loosely be grouped into 7 key categories: Global, Identity, Values, Rules, Experiential, Neurological wiring & Situational.

Again, an acronym - GIVENS - because we might say "Isn't that a given?" when they are challenged.

And, Yes, I realise that GIVENS only has 6 letters, but the Rules sneak in next to values and really warrant being their own category.

In this section, we're going to focus on how to uncover Global and Identity beliefs as these are the simplest and most powerful influencers on our willingness to take action.

If you want to learn more about the other layers of GIVENS, you will find them in the courses in the "From Within" section at: wisteriaenterprises.com.au/resources

Any activity that doesn't align with our beliefs will require more energy. Using comedy as an example, challenging the identity belief - "I'm not funny" took lots and lots of energy on my part.

That belief was backed by experiential beliefs - plenty of references of telling a joke and being reprimanded instead of laughed with. Though even with all the evidence I had it still didn't mean it was true.

I probably layered some Global beliefs in there as well. Women aren't funny. Mums need to be serious. Presenters need to be professional. Blah, blah, blah. All those GIVENS being challenged took a lot of my psychological energy.

Using some sentence starters, we can easily uncover some of our givens. This will help identify how much energy you will need to exert to take action. The more they are misaligned with your desired outcome the more energy you'll require until you're able to change them.

Global Beliefs - these are generalisations about groups of people or things we find in the world. How you finish the following sentences will help you understand how much energy you might need to approach cleaning with your family.

When it comes to cleaning men are ...

When it comes to cleaning women are ...

When it comes to cleaning kids are ...

You may find you have a couple of answers for each. That's okay. Take note of them somewhere.

You may also want to substitute in wives/husbands/

parents or any other titles or labels you apply to yourself or the people you live with.

Some other generalisations you may want to unpack that will impact your willingness to create a home you love include:

Decluttering is ...

Decluttering means ...

Declutters (people who declutter) are ...

If I declutter, then ...

Decluttering makes me ...

Decluttering gives me...

You may also want to substitute any other words you associate with household management. For example: cleaning, tidying, organising, managing, leadership, parenting, and so many others.

At this point you should have a nice long list of Global beliefs. And while they may look daunting, they are all within your control to change.

Next, we are going to look at Identity statements, they can be identified by using sentences that include "I am ..."

Using your words above finish this sentence:

When it comes to decluttering, I am ...

Then ask what else at least three times.

Again, substitute in various other household management tasks you want to undertake. You can even just play by starting a sentence with the words I am and seeing what you discover.

At this point you should have a nice long list of beliefs. You now have a choice. You can try and change those beliefs so you can take action, which as a coach I endorse as coaching is a great way to challenge beliefs. Or, if you want the faster track, you can simply acknowledge they are stories, they are not facts, and you can take action to bring other possibilities to life.

TASK: *Look over your relationships lists closely and see if any beliefs are holding you back from creating a home you love.*

Put a star next to the ones you are ready to let go.

Identify an action that would prove that belief to be untrue and go do it.

Of course, if you aren't willing to take action, the action route won't work. At which point, I recommend a coach to support you. Who at some point, will recommend you take action to cement the change in your beliefs.

It's your call, you can do this the slow and long way (which I myself have chosen more than once) or you can do this the quick and simple way. Neither is easy. Neither is comfortable all the time. You choose. Long or Hard. Of course, you can always choose neither, but if you want to create a home you love (and you haven't already) I promise you some of your beliefs and actions will need to change.

My apologies, that's not a more upbeat and positive message, but I am a pragmatic coach and author, not a feel-good one.

When it comes to transformation the best way to feel more inspired, more alive, is to take action towards your dreams (even if it challenges one or more of your beliefs).

Of course, there is so much more depth we could go into around the topic of connecting with our hearts. If you want to learn more about the various ways we can explore more deeply our psychological energy, the archetypes influence on us, the relationships you have with people and tasks and your thinking be sure to check out some of my other books and courses that focus on making changes "From Within", for now, you have enough to continue focusing on making changes at home.

Step 3: Discover what the Experts Say

When it comes to expanding our beliefs, finding the thinking patterns, observing the archetypes' journeys, and increasing our Hope the easiest way is to look to the people who have success and what they take as GIVENS.

In this chapter we will look at three key elements of household management.

Decluttering - removing unwanted items from our home
Organising - categorising and finding homes for our stuff
Routines - maintaining the order we created

Decluttering

Over the years I've read many books, signed up to a number of programs, got countless emails all on this topic.

My first introduction to the concept was in 2004 when I had my first child and my Mum introduced me to Flylady. She taught a slow and steady approach to decluttering - just do 15 minutes at a time. But she didn't really bring a system or strategy into my awareness.

My next encounter was in the declutter fad when the KonMari book hit the stores. I was sold - following Flylady's 15 minutes a day for 15 (or so) years had taken its toll and I was ready to take massive action - and that is what Marie Kondo recommends in her book.

Dive in, dive hard, and get each category done quickly so you can then move to the maintaining phase. Ask yourself if it brings you Joy and remove anything that doesn't. It took me three weeks to follow this method (and burn myself out in the process).

These extremes both had value to me and my journey of reducing the amount of stuff in my home, but the game changer when it comes to decluttering in terms of an ideology and a system was Dana from "A slob comes clean".

She introduced me to two really key concepts that I found as philosophies were game changing. They are the Clutter Threshold and the Container Concept.

Clutter threshold

Our Clutter threshold or inventory levels are about how much stuff we can manage. Clutter is an item that doesn't have a consistent home and takes up space that is allocated to something else (be it another item, or simply physical or mental space).

There are two components in play here.

The physical capabilities of managing inventory and our emotional/mental capacity related to managing our possessions.

Many people have a desire to be busy as proof that they have a level of function and purpose in their lives. Some people direct that energy towards managing stuff. The higher the need to feel needed the more stuff is accumulated to fuel that need to be needed.

The more comfortable we become in the stillness and spaciousness the less stuff is required.

I look at this as a spectrum. Too much at one end, too little at the other, and the Goldilocks zone in the middle that's just right.

Everyone will have their own version of this. And it's not fixed. Our desire to fill our lives with stuff or to get rid of our stuff is in constant flux. This is because it is rarely a logical choice, and more an emotional one.

Some days I love the starkness of my bedroom. Other days it feels bare and barren. Some days I can bring gratitude for the abundance of clothes I have. Other days I feel like I'm buried under the burden. There will however be a general space where we can hit the just right mark.

As we look to declutter there needs to be a balance between the physical capabilities of managing our possessions and the emotional attachments connected to stuff.

Sadly, there's no fast-track quiz to uncover our threshold. It's something to bring awareness to in your day-to-day reflections.

Emotionally - You will know you have reached your ideal inventory when there is no longer a sense of pressure, burden, and obligation from the silent todo list, instead you feel calm, organised, & replenished by your home.

Logically you will know you have reached your ideal inventory when everything has a home & you and your family can maintain putting items away in your day-to-day busy life.

Which leads us nicely to the next thought that Dana from "A Slob comes Clean" on YouTube introduced me to and that is the Container Concept.

Dana has a great video on her YouTube Channel where she explains this you can check it out here: https://www.youtube.com/watch?v=_24PoIZSmVs

The Container Concept

The simplicity of this as to making decisions about what to keep and what to let go astounds me.

Her viewpoint is that everything is a container, including our homes. I mean we could expand this perspective to the world, the world is a container, and within it are other containers. Kind of like nesting dolls in a way. The smaller ones fit within the larger ones. Unlike nesting dolls there can be multiple shaped and sized containers within the larger containers.

So, in our homes, we have rooms, each of these is a container. We have kitchens, bedrooms, bathrooms, and living spaces.

Within each of these we have containers. We have shelves, cupboards, chests, drawers etc. And in them we have containers, jars, boxes, shelves, dividers, etc.

Items live in the containers. For example, one of the items I love is books. And while I value Konmari's question of "Do I love it?" when it comes to books my answer is almost always Yes. Which meant I'd end up with more books than I can comfortably fit within my clutter threshold if this was all I asked.

What the container concept adds into the mix is the key question - do I have space for this?

Now, books, ideally, in my house, live on a bookshelf, but there are a finite number of shelves. Now of course I could always buy another set of shelves, which are then placed against walls in one of my rooms - again though there are a finite number of walls.

We can use our wall space as the guide, or container, for how many bookshelves we own. The shelves then become the guide for how many books we can own.

This takes the emotionality out of decluttering and makes the amount of space in the container the deciding factor.

When I buy a new book, I need to ensure it fits on the shelves. If it doesn't then I need to make a choice - which book stays and which goes. The container dictates how many books I keep - not my love for books.

When we have more books than shelves, we can then use priorities to help choose which ones we keep. By using an A/B choice system. Our new book that is looking for a home needs to replace a book on the shelf. As we look at the existing books, we ask ourselves if we want to keep the new book more or less than the book on the shelf.

If the answer is more, we take out the old book and replace it with the new book. We then continue to do the process with the new book until we get all the way along the shelf and the book, we are holding is wanted less than every other book on the shelf. We may still want it, however if we use the space criteria the answer is No. And so, it leaves.

We can fit as much or as little as we want in our house, but we are always choosing between what we want more and less. We can choose if we want more walls on which to hang pictures or more bookshelves. We can choose between wanting more stuff or more space.

As a Bee (we'll discuss what that means exactly in the next section) I love to see my knowledge on the wall. It delights me. Marie Kondo, most likely a Cricket, preferring visual simplicity, prefers her books to be in a kindle app (or so I've been led to believe).

Our preference for visual abundance or simplicity impacts our emotional/mental space. This also becomes a factor when considering the container concept. How many items our brain is willing to put in a space creates our perception of the item's 'happiness'.

How many books can you see happily living together on a shelf?

For me - the answer is LOTS. I'm happy to have bookshelves take up most of the wall space in my office, the hall, and my kid's rooms. My mind has capacity for this visual stimulation (with the things I love).

In a nutshell, using the container concept comes down to three simple steps.

Identify the item you are assessing

Choose the container parameters

Only keep what fits 'happily' in that space

TASK: *Pay attention to which question lights you up more when it comes to decluttering - is it asking if something brings you joy or does it fit in the space?*

Also consider which of those questions is going to be more effective in helping you create the home you love?

There's really no right or wrong here, it's simply what works better for you.

Now let's expand on what I mean by Bee and Cricket and discover the other Clutterbug organising styles.

Organising

Again, over the years I've come across many organising experts, but none spoke to my heart quite like Cas Aarson from Clutterbug.

The Clutterbug philosophy starts off by saying: "Organising isn't one size fits all, there are four different organising types. I call them Clutterbugs."

It aligns so well with my philosophy that there is NO one size fits all for ANYTHING. And there's a profile. It's no surprise that I love her. I love her so much that I took her course and am a Certified Organisational Specialist™ as a result.

The most common issue people who have taken the test come to me with is confusion because they don't quite fit the box. This is because it gives a single result. If you choose to take it, I encourage you to take note of your answers so you can give yourself a percentage score instead of a single boxed-in score. I also invite you to consider that different spaces will be approached with different styles.

In my own home I am a Crick-a-bug (a blend of cricket and lady-bug) in my bedroom while I am a Butter-bee (Butterfly + Bee) in the kitchen and my office.

These are combination types. And I think it is more realistic for most people to consider themselves as a combination.

What I love about it, is it really hones in on two key factors, our preference for Visual abundance or simplicity and our preference for macro or micro sorting.

The four bugs can be summarised as follows:
Butterfly: Visual and Macro
Bee: Visual and Detailed
LadyBug: Hidden and Macro
Cricket: Hidden and Detailed.

We'll unpack more of what that means in the next few paragraphs, but if you want to do the online profile first you can find it at: https://clutterbug.me/cas-aarssen

Many of the big name organisers are hidden organisers. My experience was that everyone I followed (including Cas) was a hidden organiser.

Marie Kondo is most likely a Cricket - wanting everything tucked away neatly and highly meticulously sorted.

Flylady is probably a LadyBug - a more macro approach, but still wanting things hidden.

This meant I often felt less than, or wrong, when I wanted to be able to see my things. What I loved when I encountered Cas was the relief that I wasn't broken or faulty, I finally accepted I just organise differently.

I have a preference for Visual Abundance (everywhere except my bedroom where I prefer Visual simplicity).

So, what does all of this mean? Let's look at the preference of hidden (visual simplicity) vs visual (abundance) organising.

The difference here is around how we store items.

Whether we want them in the open so we can easily see them or prefer them behind closed doors or in boxes so they are hidden.

There's no right or wrong, it's simply a preference.

There's also sometimes situational answers. So perhaps in the bedroom you prefer a more hidden approach and in the kitchen a more open approach. That's my preference. Clothes are hidden in drawers and wardrobes. But food is in clear containers and it's highly unusual unless I'm in a video conference that the cupboard doors are closed.

Now we will explore the second piece of the clutterbug profile, our sorting style.

Big Fish, Little Fish, Cardboard box

We all have a tendency to sort things a certain way. Maybe it's the grouping items together through the lens of the bigger picture for you, or you get down into the details, or perhaps you think in categories.

Big Fish, Little Fish, Cardboard box, as a metaphor comes from me learning this at a time when I had a child who very much loved the song by Bob the Builder.

If you're not familiar with it you can find it YouTube.

www.youtube.com/watch?v=SD1ENnVnMXM

WARNING: It is super catchy, likely to get stuck in your head, and can be very repetitious.

Big Fish = Abstract, Bigger Picture, Purpose. Heart.

Little Fish = Finer details. Movement and Experiences

Cardboard Box = Joining the two together and wrapping it all up. Operations.

The reason I loved the song Big Fish, Little Fish, Cardboard Box as a way to remember this is three-fold.

1. It's super catchy and easy to remember.
2. It goes from Big to Little, then wraps up in a cardboard box.
3. The repetition, which is how we need to do this ourselves. These things are not a single effort thing, we do Big Fish, Little Fish, wrap them together in a Cardboard Box. Then repeat. Then repeat.

TASK: *Take a look at an area in your house that you use often and is working well.*
Are your items out, easy to see or are they hidden?
Are there larger or smaller groupings of items?
This will give you a sense of your Clutterbug preferences.

Larger groups of items = Category Simplicity – Abstract.
Smaller groups of items = Category Abundance – Detailed.

Neither preference, whether more detailed or abstract is right or wrong, and neither influences our capabilities. We can all be more detail focused or more abstract in any moment, we simply have a preference, a default setting as such. Just as we can customise the washing machine despite its default setting, we can choose to look at things from another angle.

Being able to dance between the bigger picture, details, and categories means that we can approach thinking from a number of angles. We can connect to the Heart (bigger picture) the Operations (mid-level and holding our big picture and finer details together) and Movement & Experiences (finer details).

You can also increase your self-awareness of your category preference through reviewing your task or options lists:

If you've got a list a mile long (or maybe several pages) then you are most likely to be detail focused.

If you've got a shorter list of categories, with few finer details, you're more likely to land somewhere in the middle.

If you've got a very short or bigger picture list, you're more likely to be big picture, abstract, focused.

When creating lists we want to be able to dance between all three levels. Having an idea of the bigger picture, knowing the categories we can sort into, and being able to look at the finer details to take action on.

When it comes to sorting our stuff, we want to stick to our preference and what we are able and willing to maintain. Too often people set themselves up with highly detailed systems that don't fit into the daily maintenance abilities.

By knowing our preference, and the alternatives, we can create a more rounded experience for ourselves.

Our day-to-day preference is highly linked to the level of complexity we are willing and able to maintain.

A great example of the difference is my husband and I, and how we view sorting food.

Michael has three categories. Fridge, freezer, cupboard.

I have about 20, maybe more.

I'm far more specific about where items are placed within the fridge. Michael is pleased if they get in the fridge.

While he's open to live with my more detailed approach to organising, the maintenance required is more effort than he is willing to put in consistently.

The same thing happens when it comes to sorting clothes. My willingness for detailed maintenance levels, for the most part, are significantly higher. I like my clothes folded neatly and precisely. I'm okay with taking extra time to put things away. Michael prefers easy to put away and is willing to spend longer looking for items.

Navigating who is responsible for which spaces helps us decide on how much detailed organising is in place.

The kitchen which is communal we aim for broad categories and visual solutions, that everyone, even our kids is capable of maintaining. .

In the bedroom I take the time to maintain the detailed and hidden style.

Start paying attention to the number of categories you have, and the ability of yourself and your family to maintain them.

Anyone can set up a highly detailed, intricate system, once. The key, when it comes to creating a home you love, is can you (and other household members) maintain that level of detail on a day-to-day basis.

Maintaining

Maintaining is really all about action. And as such it gets given a lot of focus in the Operations and the Movement sections as well as here in the Heart.

From the perspective of our hearts, I want to look at our relationship with problem solving and how easily we come up with alternative solutions. To do this effectively and efficiently we need to look from multiple perspectives easily.

To do this we are going to start with a simple perspective taking framework called the Disney Strategy. It's been said Walt Disney had a strategy that involved moving ideas through 3 perspectives, the dreamer, the analyst, and the skeptic.

What often happens is we have a default to one of these preferences and don't let the others come to life. Maybe your skeptic shows up before the dreamer has fully expressed. Or maybe the analyst pokes holes into the dreams. Or maybe the dreamer overshadows the others, and nothing ever gets done. Or maybe everything is analysed with no clear purpose or dream in mind.

Today we are going to play with embracing all three.

A while back I noticed a frustration around the size of our

house, the constant bickering because the kids are in the same rooms and on top of each other in a single living space...

And so, I started to dream. With no holding back. If I could solve this right now, what are my options:

First thought, get rid of the kids.

Second thought, run away and never be seen again.

Third thought, rent somewhere while we wait for extensions.

This one I started to play through and dream a bit bigger. I found a 6-bedroom house with six bathrooms. It was amazing. I pictured myself living there. The kids. So much space and freedom. I kept dreaming until there was nothing left I could add in.

Then I let the analyst come in - could we afford it financially? Potentially. A couple of other logical type thoughts and questions. Working towards how we would make it work.

Then I let the skeptic in - first thought - who's cleaning all those bathrooms? Not me!! Second thought - do you really want to pour $700 a WEEK! into someone else's mortgage? No thanks.

Okay, back to the drawing board...

We could buy a house.

So back to realestate.com I headed.

And there it was... 6 bedrooms, 3 bathrooms, 2 kitchens (not sure why I needed that, but awesome). I dreamed of being there.

Then when I finished dreaming, the analyst came in. What do we need for this to work?

Bus-stop close by. Check. :) Budget within our means - Check. Anything else... A few other small logistics, solved.

We would need to go look at it to make a final choice - so I called the real-estate, and someone else had already made an offer.

Back to the drawing board...

More trawling realestate.com, nothing else caught my eye.

Back to the drawing board...

If I'm not renting, and I'm not buying, and I'm not burning the place down and claiming insurance, and I'm not getting rid of them or running away, what other options can I dream about?

We could rearrange rooms. (I hear my husband's voice in my head groan, I ignore that) and start dreaming.

If we move it like this... and we place it like that...
(It's all coming back to me now... And I go off on a tangent singing Celine Dion...)

I mapped it all out. Dreamed a bit more. :) I find myself hoping I can find a magic wand and the extensions are done.

I come back to reality a little, and re-dream what we can do this week, now, while hubby is home. I draw up a plan.

I let the analyst, armed with tape measure, come to life.

I didn't bother accessing my own critic, I went to my husband and let him loose. LOL. And, surprisingly because he'd been a part of my other thoughts that hadn't been executed, he actually jumped on board pretty fast (there's a lesson there, take ALL dreams, ALL ideas, to partners so they can see you are using ALL 3 of the Disney perspectives).

And so, we put into action my plan. The house is being shuffled as I write this and by next week when the kids are on holidays they will each have a space that is their own that they can retreat to, they will have access to THREE family areas with tech separated. I felt happy and fulfilled. I put Hope into Action. We took one step closer to creating the home I love.

So, let's recap, the three perspectives.

The dreamer is free, anything goes, all ideas are tabled.

The Analyst works out HOW to do it, how to make it work, what's required logistically (Time, Money, Energy).

The Skeptic identifies possibly hurdles, obstacles, then sends back to the Analyst to find a way or the idea gets discarded and we go back to the dream board.

Disney had different rooms/locations for each self to operate in, if you've got space, this is a great idea. If not, you could wear hats, or use different chairs as you learn how to fully embrace each of the selves within.

Using your dreamer and analyst, think about how you might approach some of your tasks.

(Dreamer) What are your options?

(Analyst) What resources will you need? Time, Money, Energy, Art of persuasion, Communication skills).

(Critic) Then, rather than letting your own critic be what talks you out of it and tables hurdles, go to the person you seek help from and see what they want to table as options and the obstacles to overcome.

If it doesn't land, go back to dreaming, then analyse, then seek someone else to help, and let them be the critic.

If your own inner critic pipes up and it's relevant, table it in that conversation and work together with the other person to resolve it.

TASK: *Use the dreamer, Analyst, and Critic perspective right now to put together your own philosophies on decluttering, organising, and maintaining your home.*

Look over your notes from the exercise in The Heart of the Matter – which perspective was in play – the dreamer, the analyst, or the skeptic?

If you looked through another perspective how does that impact the pieces of your HEART? Does Hope go up or down? Does Energy increase or decrease? Which archetypes come out to play? What relationships change? What new ways of Thinking or beliefs appear?

Part 2: Operations

In this section we will explore systems and processes to help you create a home you love.

These will provide the foundations for you to create Routines, Expectations, Agenda's, Daily Intentions, and Your Checklists. It is how you ensure you are READY to take Action.

These are not rules, they are guides. Use what works, allow yourself to ignore what doesn't align for you.

Step 4 Make decisions in advance

One of the most common obstacles people encounter when they go to declutter their homes or aim to get organised is Decision Fatigue. Symptoms can include overwhelm, frustration, guilt, brain fog, procrastination, a sense that it is all too hard, and so much more.

Pushing through when we feel fatigued will take us to burnout. At which point we can no longer continue. We want to ensure we notice when we are reaching a point of decision fatigue and set ourselves up to overcome and prevent it from getting worse.

Have you ever had a day where even deciding what flavour tea to drink was a burden? I have. That moment where someone asks, "What's for dinner?" and you just want to fall apart, break down and cry because it all seems too much.

Every day we are making hundreds of micro decisions. Should I get up or hit snooze? Half flush or full flush? Does the kettle need more water before I boil it? Blog post or dishwasher first? Is this clean enough to wear again? What needs washing most? And that's all in the first ten minutes of waking up. And so it continues...

No wonder that within an hour or two we start to find it harder to make choices. Add in something more intense, like decluttering, and without a grounded guide it is no wonder so many give up or burn out.

So, what can we do to overcome (and prevent) decision fatigue?

Overcoming Decision Fatigue

There are three things we can do to limit decision fatigue.

1. Have Support.
2. Notice Successes
3. Develop Clear Criteria

Let's explore them each in more depth.

Support

Too often we think we need to do this alone. I don't know where or why the concept of being independent stuck, and while we do need to embrace a level of self-reliance and independence in our lives; if we look at the journey of fulfillment there are more steps, and they include developing interdependence and utilising co-regulation.

We are not meant to operate in isolation, we are designed to be members of a community, supporting, encouraging, and helping one another.

Step 1 to overcoming decision fatigue is ensuring you

have support. When I have big decisions to make, I always brainstorm them with someone else. You'll often see on my Facebook profile I'm sharing things where I need support, or I need external input.

Some people are internally driven, while others need external reflection to think. I'm an external processor through and through, and for far too many years I was told that was wrong. Now I embrace it. And I talk through my ideas with people who are able to reflect and help me find my own answers.

We all, even those of us seen as "Experts" need support. I know so many questions, I have all the criteria, the processes are embedded into a course I wrote, and still, on a big day, with hard choices, I call an accountability buddy and we chat through and she supports me to make the choices.

Notice Successes

One of the most common things that my support team does for me is remind me of my progress. One of the things we do as humans is we incorporate what is and forget what was. It's easy to spot the things we still don't have working. Our minds are programmed to look for danger, difference, and details. This is how we survive. And back in the day when we lived in caves and a blade of grass moving meant that there could be a predator about to pounce it was helpful and those who responded by taking action were kept alive more than those who were not.

However, now, we don't live in an everyday world filled with lions and tigers and bears. The dirty sock won't kill us, and yet for so many of us that is how our body reacts. Firing off all the chemicals that are designed for our survival. We respond to the difference, the out of place, as danger, and our defence mechanisms kick in.

Some of us are more prone to this than others, we amplified these protection mechanisms in our childhoods to keep us safe. Some of us have mental wiring that makes us more sensitive to these things.

When left to its natural focus, our brain will keep pointing out what is wrong, and never notice where we have made progress. When all we see is what is not working, we feel even more burdened and our mind is less able to make decisions, and we are more prone to decision fatigue.

This is why it is so important to incorporate a version of TADA lists into your life. When instead we start to focus on the successes, on the progress we have made, on the decisions we make easily and effortlessly (and there are some, we are making hundreds a day, most are unconscious), when we notice these, we start to remind ourselves that we can do this. This can be a massive turning point in our approach to any goal, including creating a home we love.

Clear Criteria

As you notice the choices you make easily, you'll find that many of them are premade and many are easy because the criteria are pre-determined. Rubbish or Recycling is not usually a hard choice because we have clear criteria. To keep or not to keep can start to be more difficult because our criteria are so often flawed or missing a key component.

Remember that "What kind of Tea?" question from earlier - I have criteria to answer this. I drink my tea (as well as many other self-care rituals) based on where I am in my menstrual and energetic cycles. Today for instance I am in Deep Luteal - so it's something calming that is required. I'm inspired and motivated, so it's something that aligns with that. Which means Spiced Apple, Cinnamon, and Camomile. Now I know many people make this even simpler and only have one kind of hot beverage they drink consistently, which works as a solution too.

When it comes to decision making there are 7 key criteria we use to make the choices to act or not, these are the ways in which we J.U.S.T.I.F.Y our decisions. 3 of these will support us to create a home we love, 3 will hold us back and keep us trapped under the mountain of stuff, and 1 could go either way. We'll talk about these soon.

First, think about how well you receive support, if you seek it when you need it, and if you are taking time to celebrate your successes.

If you haven't yet embraced creating a Daily TADA list - focused on noticing your successes, and allowing yourself to really feel that success, acknowledge the progress, and embrace that you are on the pathway to transforming your chaos, do that now.

If you aren't connecting with a community and asking for help. Expressing your needs. Do that. My online community exists so you can reach out and ask for help, seek support, and receive it. If you are not open to being helped, if you aren't expressing your needs, you'll most likely stay stuck. I'm here for you, and so are the other members of the movement. We are all in this together. There is no question too silly, no emotion we won't validate, it's okay to be vulnerable, it's okay to express your needs - if the community can meet them, it will.

I look forward to seeing your celebrations of success and your expressions of needs, openly receiving support from the group.

An unwillingness to be open and receive support is one of the most common areas people justify keeping themselves stuck. We can do things differently. Navigating past our excuses is not a journey to be taken alone. Processing emotions is not possible in isolation until we have had that emotion validated and accepted. Challenging our identity requires support and companionship.

We also often need someone outside to help us see things clearly. To point out where we are holding ourselves back. Someone to challenge us and ask:

TASK: *Identify the people in your life you can call on when you need to be supported, challenged, or encouraged.*

Are they reasons or excuses?

The fastest way we can manage our choices is with awareness of how we justify the current arrangement.

Whether it's asking for help, making a choice about what to keep and what to declutter it all comes down to having clear criteria to make a decision. We will find ourselves justifying an old pattern or keeping a possession, and without discernment, it's hard to tell if it is a valid reason, or simply an excuse.

The biggest obstacle is that both our reasons and our excuses are often valid logical conclusions. We can very elegantly justify why an excuse is valid.

The difference is that reasons are based on sound foundations, excuses are not. Genuine reasons generally make sense and are founded in reasonable sound logic and take care of our emotions.

Excuses, while they may seem valid, are often built on unsound foundations, are fueled by misconceptions, and hold us back from creating the home, and life, we love.

Reasons based on purpose include: Joy, Usefulness, & Space.

Excuses are most often focused on Time, Identity, Finances.

The three reason-based questions are commonly taught by experts for people to consider when decluttering, and can just as easily be applied to choosing a community and so many other choices we make.

1. Does it spark Joy?
2. Is it Useful now?
   If both are No, meaning it doesn't spark joy and is not useful now then out it goes, out of our house, out of our calendar, and out of our minds
   (NOTE: we'll explore what to do with ideas for later in the Planning with GRACE section of the book).
   If either of those is a Yes - then we need to consider:
3. Does it fit in the Space?

Remembering that space relates to our physical, mental, and emotional capacity.

While these questions give us a clear set of parameters, letting go of something (a task, a possession, a thought) may require you to identify and overcome the excuses on the flip of the scales.

The top 3 excuses we use to hold onto things are:

1. Time - I've had/done it for ages &/or it may be useful one day.
2. Identity - But I'm a ___ and they own/do ___

3. Finances - It cost a lot & I could make money if I sold it.

If something is hard to release but doesn't meet the first few criteria ask yourself:

Am I letting the past (I used to love this) or future (it might be useful one day) influence my choice for today?

Is who I think I need to be influencing this choice?
(Eg. I am a crafter therefore I need lots of craft supplies - perpetuated by memes like: The person with the largest stash wins)

Am I holding onto the hope that this will repay what it cost if I hold onto it longer?

Identifying where you are Justify-ing bonus Questions
You could also try:
Does this bring me Joy or drain me?
Is it Useful now?
Is it worthy of having a dedicated Space in my house, mind, or life?

And when all else fails it's time to get on the phone or jump into an online community and seek support. I have good friends, accountability buddies, group mentoring programs, and 1:1 coaches that are my lifeline when my excuses outweigh my ability to listen to my reasons. I invite and encourage you to ensure you equip yourself with the same.

Writing this book has had me call an accountability buddy, talk with a coach, leverage my husband's love for my wisdom and tap very deeply into navigating past my excuses.

My past wanted to have an opinion, and my fear of the future as well. My Identity has been challenged many times and I had to embrace even more deeply who I am as a Household Manager, a Coach, and an Author and let go of a lot of limiting identities. I also needed to overcome my misconception about if it takes me longer to write the book I will earn more money (which is soooo ludicrous being that my primary purpose in business is passion not profit!!)

I've also had to overcome these excuses getting rid of many of my possessions. My aspirational identities have all kinds of plans that buy all kinds of things (like a drawing kit that I haven't opened in 5 years). My past identities don't want to give up who I once was (like the scrapbooking supplies I didn't touch for over 5 years but struggled to let go).

This is an emotional journey. One that gets easier with practice. It's not time to go and dive into the hardest, most emotional space in your home (or life). Start with something simple and easy. Give yourself success, build momentum, and then tackle the harder items.

TASK: Practice **identifying how you are Justify-ing** *(or not) with easy things.*

Explore if you have reasons or excuses.
Joy, Usefulness, Space, (Reasons)
Time, Identity, Finances, (Excuses)
Your Preferences (Could swing either way)

Set yourself up for success in learning to trust your decisions about items in your home and life - choose things that are less likely to bring up the excuses and get no brainer answers simply from the first three questions.

For example: The rubbish on the kitchen bench.
Does it bring me Joy - No.
Is it Useful - No.

So out it goes.

Hunt for more trash, more easy, simple, No, No, items. No Joy - No Use. No more will it take up space.

Find some no Brainer Yes, Yes, Yes items as well.

For example:
My Frog hanging chain over my bed.
Does it bring me Joy - Yes
Is it Useful - Yes
Do I have Space for it - Yes

No brainer to keep.

Aim to assess your decisions on 5 items.

Again - stick with what is easy. All you are doing is proving to yourself you can make easy fast decisions when the criteria is clear. Anything that is harder, leave alone, just seek out the easy items.

The goal is to build your ability to trust your Yes and No and make decisions based on solid reasons instead of excuses.

Purpose Statement

Sometimes the criteria is easy. Sometimes our unconscious purpose will override and be clear. Other times we need to be really clear about our Aim, our Target, and what we really want. While this exercise is focused on your house, on cleaning and clutter management, you can also go beyond the household purpose statement and identify the purpose of your life as well.

Our Household Purpose statement is determined by the emotions we want to feel in our home.

As we've already discussed, while we want to believe we are making logical choices, and sometimes we are, so much of what we do is driven by our emotions. If we can uncover how we want to feel we can create a criteria based on emotions, that we can then incorporate in with our logic.

We are all logical and deductive in moments. We are also all emotional and irrational at times. When we can navigate both sides of ourselves in making choices, we close the gap between who we think we are and who we truly are. We are a world of contradictions.

We've already spoken to the logical mind a lot in the preceding content. Now it's time to tap into the emotional side.

When you look around your home, how do you want to feel?

Use the advanced question guide below if you need help to find the language.

Once you have identified the emotions, create a Statement following one of the examples as a guide.

Eg 1: My House...

My house allows me to see, hear, feel and know that it's okay for me to experience (Feeling word), (Feeling word), and (Feeling word).

Mine used to read:

My house allows me to see, hear, feel and know that

it's okay for me to experience Passion, Alignment, and Joy.

Eg. 2: Individual

I (NAME) see, hear, feel and know that my house is a place of ...., & .... that supports me to .....

I, Amy, see, hear, feel and know that my house is a place of love and laughter that supports me to be Creative.

Eg. 3: Collective (Highly advanced)

We, the Grantham family, agree that our house is a place of ..., ..., & ... so we can ...

We, the Grantham Family, agree that our house is a place of connection and compassion so we can make our mark on the world.

At this point do not overthink. This is potentially a GOAL, not yet reality. Dream.

You don't need it to be original, allow yourself to take inspiration from others. If Calm, Peace and Joy are your words, let's rock forth together. If someone else has posted passionate, or connected, or loving, or kind, and they resonate, use them.

It only needs to resonate and light you up inside. If it doesn't land the first time, all good, allow it to develop over time.

Once you have your purpose statement, write it down and put it somewhere you will see it often.

If the prompts were all you needed and you've got a statement that doesn't include 'not' and 'un...' in the words rock forth. If you need some more support to help make this happen for yourself, keep reading.

One of the most common patterns in the human race is an ability to know what we don't want (moving away), identified in the use of not, and un's. Many people don't know how to put into language what they do want (moving towards). Too many of us get tied up in 'nots' focusing on what we are seeking to let go or get away from. By focusing on what we don't want, we tend to create more of it, or not break past the obstacles holding us back from reaching what we truly desire.

The metaphor I often use with my VIP 1:1 clients is that of a rocket ship.

If someone is sitting on earth proclaiming that they don't want to be on earth, they can jump, or build little rockets that momentarily take them away from earth. Gravity is strong though and without a clear desire beyond moving away from earth we rarely manage to notice it and overcome the obstacle it provides.

If instead we know we want to move away from earth, and

get to the moon, we will notice the obstacle of gravity in the way and start to be able to devise ways to overcome it.

Maybe we won't reach the moon, but if we aim for it, we will land among the stars.

Getting clearer on what we are aiming for, what we do want, allows us to notice what is in the way and devise a plan to move forward.

Some examples of moving away from language could be:

1. I don't want a messy house.
2. Well, they wouldn't be so annoying.
3. I don't want to be poor.
   D. I'd feel unstressed

The key is the words that convey 'lack' or what we don't want.

The contrast to the above statements with moving towards language might look something like:

1. I feel calm, at peace, and content in my clean, tidy, well-organised space.
2. They listen, respect me, and I feel understood and valued.
3. I am abundant in all areas of my life, physical health, relationships, mentally, spiritually and financially.
4. I'd feel free and light

To make the shift, linguistically, from focusing on what we don't want to what we do want can take a little persistence and requires some exploratory questions.

The ones I like are:

If you didn't have (insert thing), what would you have instead?

Sometimes that may come back with another 'not' word, simply ask the above again until you get a statement that doesn't have the 'lack' focused words. It is a clear moving towards statement.

Then to get even more clear, we can go up into the abstract a little further.

What would (the new thing) give you?

For what purpose do you want (the new thing)?

I do this on repeat for a little while swapping in questions until I land somewhere really abstract, like love, or universalness, or oneness, or ultimate connection.

Eg. (S = statement, Q = question)

S - I don't want a messy house.

Q - If you didn't have a messy house, what would you have instead?

S - Well I wouldn't have lazy children.

Q - And if you didn't have lazy children, what would you have?

S - I might have better communication skills.

(Note: My answer really deviates away from the initial discussion, so I choose to bring back my focus to my house... This is advanced, but you guys can handle it).

Q - What else, what would you have in relation to your house?

S - I'd have a system and a structure to follow.

Q - What would a system and structure give you?

S - Something to guide my children and husband with.

Q - And for what purpose would you want to guide them?
S - To access more peace and calm.
Q - And what's the gift in more peace and calm?
S - Sense of fulfilment
Q - And what's the gift in a sense of fulfilment
S - I feel better
Q - and as you feel better, what is the gift in that?
S - More connection to myself.
Q - And as you experience more connection with self, what does that give you?
S - A sense of peace.
(Note the loop back to an answer, this is normal!)
Q - And as you have more peace, available to you, whole and complete, what's the gift in that for you?
(Advanced question, rock forth with it, it's pretty awesome if I do say so myself)
S - Oneness. A deep sense of oneness.

Then I enjoy that feeling for a moment. Breathe it in. And backtrack to capture what I really want. Which from the above is:

More connection to myself. Through creating fulfilment, using a system and structure to guide myself and my kids, to a place of peace and calm.

Good thing I'm sharing this system and structure and reconnecting with it again myself. ;)

TASK: *Decide what is it you want from your house and create a Purpose Statement*

Step 5 Using EASE and GRACE to make PLANS

One of the greatest challenges I've noticed that many people face when making decisions about paperwork, digital files, or possessions is that they have little to no criteria on how to decide what to do, which can leave them confused, overwhelmed, or sometimes frustrated.

Something like checking emails becomes a long and tiring process, because each time they open one and see an action could be required, they feel compelled to do something with it straight away, they then need to get caught in overthinking wondering what to do, or an action whirlwind, doing doing doing, caught in the busyness of taking care instead of taking care of their business.

Whether in an office setting or at home, we all have business to take care of, there are bills to pay, chores to do, children to run after, so many things that take up our attention. The benefit of predetermining how we intend to make our decisions about what we find in emails, messages or other forms of input like a crying cat means that instead of worrying about how we will decide on each individual message, we can focus on following a process.

When we utilize task lists, project plans, and a calendar, we can create a way more efficient and effective way of managing our time, energy, and effort. As a result, you will get more of what matters done in a timely and effective fashion, giving you more time to chill out doing things like taking a bubble bath, hanging out in nature, or taking a nap.

Deciding with Ease

In the last section we talked about making decisions in advance. When it comes to sorting paperwork, managing emails, even closing tabs in an internet browser, too many people are easily overwhelmed. And I get it, I'm the first to admit that opening my email has been known to create feelings of anxiety. Looking at the 27 tabs I have opened can easily take me to a state of panic. Decision fatigue would kick in before I even started. We, (okay maybe I), tell ourselves that there are too many options and choices. This is a lie.

The truth is, whether we are sorting emails, closing tabs, or clearing off the kitchen bench, as we assess each item and decide how to handle it, there are only ever 4 options available to us. When we understand this, we remove the need to survey the options, to overcomplicate the process, and we allow ourselves to focus. While we have masses of information coming in, we know that how we respond will only ever be one of these 4 options. Narrowing our focus to 4 options is simple, easy, effective, and efficient.

When facing an input, whether physical, digital, or mental, we always have the same four outcomes to choose from. We can make our choice with EASE.

The four options are:
Execute - Take action
Allocate - Schedule a time to handle it
Store - File the information for a later time
Erase - Remove the information from our life and mind

That's it.

Using this system, we look at our emails and we can either take action, schedule a task or appointment, file the email for later, or delete it.

Or we survey the kitchen bench and find numerous items. Each of them however can be handled by using the four options.
Dishes - we either wash them (execute), move them to the sink to be washed later (allocate), we put them away (store), or we bin them (delete).
Mail/Notes - we open them, if action is required, we take or schedule it. If it only contains information, we either file them (store) or we bin them (erase).

Perhaps you are on a call or in a class and you need to choose how to respond to what you are hearing. The same 4 options apply.
You hear something that inspires you and you take action. (Execute)
You hear something that you need to handle later you add it to a task list or your calendar (Allocate)
You hear something you want to remember that doesn't need

action and you take a note (Store).

You hear stuff that while nice really has no implications for you - you allow it to flow through your mind and move on (in essence Erasing it).

The reason we end up overwhelmed is not because there are too many options (though we often tell ourselves that), it's because we opt not to make choices. We ignore the pizza box on the bench and defer the decision. We pick up the mail, decide it's too hard and put it back down on the bench.

Deferred decisions, those we put off till later, are our biggest enemy. We often defer or put off making decisions because we have overcomplicated the process. We defer decisions because we don't want to feel the cognitive dissonance between who we say we are and who we truly are. We make up stories about who we want to be and defer making choices that align with who we truly are.

There is an episode of "How I met your Mother" where two of the main characters, Ted and Marshall, keep deferring decisions. They encounter a choice they don't want to make, and they say, "That's future Ted and Marshalls' problem" this is what we are doing too, every time we see something and don't Execute, Allocate, Store, or Erase we say to ourselves "That's Future Me's Problem".

By deferring decisions, we place more pressure on ourselves tomorrow. And the problem is that today is yesterday's tomorrow. By not taking care of today we create a future for ourselves that has more to handle than it warrants. When we simplify our decision-making process and limit how much we allocate (even unconsciously) to tomorrow, we make fewer choices because we don't keep making choices about the same item over and over again. This leads to us having more space for fulfillment and joy in our lives.

When we encounter an input (whether physical, digital, or mental) there really are only these 4 options. To determine which of the options is the best choice we only need to ask ourselves a few simple questions.

Our first question - Does it require Action?

If the answer is yes, we have Action based input.

If the answer is no, we have Information-based input.

Action-based input has two options - do something now (Execute) or do something later (Allocate).

Information-based input has two options - file it so we can find it later (Store) or remove the information from our lives and minds (Erase)

In some instances, we will have information that is both Action and Information based. In these cases, we are still faced with the 4 options. We start with the action options, then move onto the information options.

To make a choice about if we take action or we allocate we simply need to ask ourselves: "Can action be taken right now, where we are?" If it can - do it. If it can't - allocate it - to a task list or to your calendar.

To choose which option applies in the case of an information-based input the question is: "Will it be needed later?"

If the answer is no, we can delete (erase) that input and our reflection on that particular input is complete.
If the answer is yes, we need to then file the input.

Common filing locations could include things like current projects, future projects, reference materials, and resources.

The most important piece here is to not allow yourself to answer, "I don't know". While that may seem true, if it's not a No, it's a Yes. If it's not a Yes, it's a No.

When asking ourselves if an item needs us to take action the answer is Yes, or No. In this case "I don't know" probably means No. If the action is not clear, it doesn't need action. Actions are clear instructions; we know instantly what we need to do in response to an Action-based input.

If there is doubt, the most likely probability is you have an Information Input.

The exception to this is when you know action needs to be taken, but you aren't certain of the action you need to take, or perhaps the action needs to be taken by someone else. In this instance your first action is to create a plan that identifies your first action step. Making the plan can be done instantly or it can be allocated.

When you choose to create the plan you then need to assess if you can do that step. Now if the answer is yes, do it. If you still encounter an "I don't know" challenge, it means your first step was too big or unclear. If you get stuck in an "I don't know" and are unable to take action because your steps are too ambiguous, your first action needs to be identifying someone you can ask for help. If you have a limiting belief around asking for help, now is your moment to release it and embrace that no one can do this alone, we all need help at some times.

TASK: *Assess if the decisions with EASE formula works for you. Rename the categories if it helps you connect with it more. Practice making choices using the key questions.*

Getting organised with GRACE

Many years ago, I read the book Getting Things Done by David Allen and there were a few stand out ideas. One of the biggest moments of transformation was inspired by the quote: "Your mind is for having ideas, not holding them."

Too often we are seeking creativity, inspiration, innovation, all of the wonderful things our mind can do, while filling our mind with other focus points. Using our brain as a storage facility decreases its capacity to operate at its full potential. If we are using a computer with 38 tabs and apps open (something I may or may not have a lot of experience with...) it will run slower. To make it run faster we need to clear the cache, we need to let the clipboard be erased, and we need to close some of the active items. Our brains are the same. When we have 3000 things that we are aiming to remember we slow down our capacity for innovation and creativity.

I know I shared this quote earlier, but it is so relevant I'm going to share Matthew McConaughey's wise words again. "I don't write things down to remember, I write them down so I can forget"

In the book Getting things done by David Allen he outlines a simple system for ensuring we have a method to get ideas out of our minds, but have them available to access when we need them again. He calls this "GTD". I call it GRACE. This acronym was inspired by his work.

There are five simple steps in the organising with GRACE system.
Gather.
Reflect.
A List for Everything.
Come Back
Engage

Step one is to gather all your inputs together. If it's a spontaneous input, you want to gather into a contained input.

Step two, is to reflect on each input either as they come in, or as we have scheduled our time to review our lists and our contained inputs.

Step three, we create a list for everything and everything important goes on a list. We create reminders and checklists so that we know whether we're on track.

Step four, we come back and review and reflect on those lists as often as needed to keep our minds clear.

Step five, we engage with our lists as required, taking action is absolutely key for success and fulfillment.

Gathering our inputs.

There is so much information and stuff we have coming into our lives, our minds, and our homes. There are two main kinds of inputs. Free range and Captured. Free-range inputs are easily lost, and difficult to find again. Captured inputs are contained, they are documented in some way, and are easy to find if we have a filing system.

Free-range inputs include things such as random thoughts, notes on paper scraps, telephone calls, text messages, unsorted voice notes, or open tabs in an internet browser. Keeping track of them is difficult.

Captured inputs are easily able to be sorted or searched. Things such as emails, task lists, or calendars. These are easy to search and find the information we need. An extension of these can be well-kept notes in a notebook or an online app like Asana.

Ideally, we want to Reflect on input and ensure that any essential free-range inputs are either acted on instantly or captured so we can come back and engage with them later.

Reflect

Whenever a new input comes in we reflect and make a decision. The decide with EASE model we discussed in the last section provides us with the clarity to do this quickly and efficiently.

We need to reflect on how much we can execute, where we track the items allocated, how we will store items, and how much we are willing to erase from our lives.

We talked briefly about distinguishing between what to

do now and what to do later. Now it's time to discuss more deeply how we Allocate and Store items.

And this leads to the next step in the Grace acronym.

A place for everything and everything in its place

This quote attributed to Benjamin Franklin speaks to not only our physical possessions, but also our digital files and thoughts.

My own take on this when it comes to planning and organising is "A list for everything, and everything on a List". We've already discussed a number of lists that I love. TADA lists, Options lists, and the DailyFROG lists. In the next section we are going to discuss more in depth another set of lists I love called PLANS.

For now, I am just going to remind you of some of the benefits of using lists. When we allow ourselves to take things from our minds and place them on paper we free ourselves. We allow ourselves to have a sense of peace. We feel more secure and stable. But this requires us to keep track of those lists.

There are many methods out there on how to contain, capture or otherwise gather your lists, but the key to all of them is you have a place for everything, and everything is put in its place. A place for tasks, appointments, ideas, habits, memories, and so much more.

Ryder Carroll, author of the Bullet Journal, says in his intro to the bullet journal method on youtube "I needed a system flexible enough to handle whatever I threw at it and fast enough that it wouldn't get in the way". This is what we all need. Something that is aligned with our own preferences and works for us and our unique brain wiring.

I'm not going to be presumptuous enough to outline the one-size fits all system - it's something you will need to play with and experiment with to find what works best for you. What I will do instead is to share with you three key areas that you need to consider.

Your needs
Your Categories.
Your Platform

Your Needs

What is it that you need from the system?

To answer this question you will need to consider your current life areas that require planning and organising, where do you have responsibilities, where are you required to be aware of and on top of actions and information. How many areas do you need to address?

You also need to consider who else needs to have access. For example, my own system needs to navigate a few key areas of my life.

As well as managing my household I run a business (actually 2, with intentions of running a 3rd shortly), in this space there are a lot of things I need to be on top of, and I also need to communicate effectively with my team - my co-facilitator, my clients, my virtual assistant.

I am also a member of the local guide support group which requires me to take some actions and also coordinate with other members of the group. My kids attend 2 different schools and bring home information for me to coordinate with their teachers. I could go on, but you get the idea.

Each of these areas of life have various needs, for myself, and those I need to connect with must be considered as I create my management systems.

Focusing on home management you need to consider how much you want to be doing things, giving reminders, and how much you want to set up members of your family to embrace an interdependence which requires clear communication.

When I used to go away often and my mother in law came to watch my kids I needed to be able to easily and effectively communicate with her and empower my kids to access the information they needed while I was away. This meant I needed clear, simple, easy to access documentation.

Your Categories

While I will share with you many acronyms in this book, which are generally the way I have categorised things, it's important that you choose categories that work for you.

If my acronyms/categories resonate and align with your way of thinking - use them, share them, please by all means. However if they don't I invite you, as I have done when learning other peoples systems, to change them to work for how you think. How you search.

Remember my story about the cardstock - alphabetical vs colour coded - we all have our preference and while I hope the acronyms I share and the way I think inspires and motivates some people, I am more than aware that we are all unique and need to choose categories on the way we sort, search, and interact with information.

My own systems are more intricate and detailed than many of my clients can be bothered doing in their lives and businesses. The key is to choose categories based on your own preferences. My desire for category abundance leads to more detailed systems. If you have a stronger preference for category simplicity please adapt to you and your needs.

Your Platform

However many categories you choose, whatever your needs, you will need to choose a platform in which to capture your lists. We all have a choice between paper or digital (or a combination of the two). We also have a choice between a single place with categories, or multiple places by category.

What I mean by that is that we can choose to have, for example, one notebook (or app) that contains ALL the different areas of our life. Bullet Journals and the Elisi App are variations of one place platforms - containing calendars, lists, projects, and space for every area of our life.

Alternatively, we can choose multiple platforms based on category. I, with my preference for complexity over simplicity, opt for this. I have a range of apps that I use for various areas of my life and I tend to sort by category first, then choose an app. Rather than the app/book first, then categories within.

There's no right or wrong, simply your preference.

TASK: *Identify your needs, categories, and platform and get clear on the place for all your lists.*

Come Back

As much as I wish it was, just writing the list is not enough. Writing down allows us to clear our mind but at some stage we need to look at the lists.

If you want to achieve success with this system it is imperative you make time to come back and look over your lists.

For some people this needs to be scheduled, perhaps using a reminder. We'll talk more about this in the upcoming section on formulating habits.

For others they have a natural propensity to come back organically and stay on top of connecting.

In terms of how often we need to come back to the lists, this will vary, both person by person, and list by list.

David Allen suggests in his book that we come back as often as needed. I find that referring to my lists can be the best thing for me to do in times of anxiety or stress, they provide me with a sense of certainty and I find them very grounding. This isn't everyone's experience. You'll need to experiment and choose when and how often you come back to look at your lists.

When we look at the lists we are getting input and we need to loop back to the Reflect step - moving each item on the list through the Decide with EASE criteria once more.

How often we want to expose ourselves to these choices will influence how often we come back to our lists.

Remember though, ignoring a list and making it future-you's problem is how we create overwhelm and risk decision fatigue when we do decide to come back to them.

Of course just looking at our lists is not enough. We also need to take action.

Engage

How effectively we engage with our lists will influence how successful this system is in helping us manage our lives.

We need to engage enough to take the imperative actions, but not so much that we are making unnecessary decisions or creating work for us.

The system is designed to help us be both productive and fulfilled. We need to be using the system, not allowing it to control us.

You will know you have hit the sweet spot between disorganised and overly rigid when you are able to navigate your life and household management with grace and ease. Of course this is a spectrum and there will be days where you feel stressed, overwhelmed, and challenged, there will be moments where things fall through the cracks, there will be moments when your desire for control has you become a version of you that you don't like. All of this is part of the journey.

What I've portrayed above is an ideal. It is the goal. It is not always going to be the reality. You are human, as am I, and everyone else. It's okay for this to be done imperfectly. Simply aim for progress. One step, one day, one list at a time.

TASK: *Decide when you will next look at your lists and engage with them, making decisions with EASE.*

Step 6 - Strategic Planning

There's a difference between Organising and Planning.

Organising is about making sure we can find what we need when we need it. And follows some kind of system. We covered this in the section on GRACE - though not everyone will follow this exact process it will contain similar elements.

Planning goes beyond simply organising. In one way it's the difference between proactive and reactive. Getting organised with Grace responds to incoming information, it is reactive.

Strategic planning is proactive - it's getting ahead of the game before we even start the game.

Of course, for most of us at least, we are already well into playing the game of life... our houses are already mismanaged, our relationships built on bad habits, and we cant just hit reset and start again.

This however is not a reason to avoid strategic planning. Mid match referees will evaluate, take stock, and give the team a strategy.

It's never too late to take back control. To become

proactive and strategic. When coupled with all you've already learned about taking care of today, connecting with your heart, discovering what others are using, making decisions in advance, and getting organised with grace, you are equipped to start to think strategically. To become even more proactive with how you approach creating a home, and life, you love.

Strategy and planning are very similar. They focus on our ideal actions and creating results.

A good plan provides an overview of the journey ahead, is inspirational, and aligns with our own unique preferences.

There are 3 Key pieces that contribute to a strategic plan:

1. It clearly shows each of the Main Pieces
   This will vary depending on the type of plan we are creating, it could include breaking a project into smaller tasks, color-coding our calendar, distinguishing between different routines in our day, or creating key categories to organise our notes.
2. It contains simple and easy Action Steps.
   One of the most common obstacles people face when using plans is that they are written in static or broad language.
   Eg. Kitchen.
   The kitchen is a room in our house, it is a static place.
   It is also a BIG category when it comes to cleaning.
   If we see broad or static language in a list or on a calendar we have to first translate it for our mind into an action.
   When we put clear action steps on our plans we don't need to translate, which is more likely to inspire us to

take action.

Eg. Wash the Dishes.

3. It uses our personal Preferences.

Planning is not one size fits all. There are 5 distinct types of plans, as well as many other preferences that influence how we plan and which plans we will engage in.

And, just like everything else we've already explored, finding which planning style suits you best is crucial to you creating a system for household management that you will love (and even more importantly will use).

5 types of Plans

Through my observation, my research, and lots of conversations with people I've uncovered the 5 different types of PLANS.

They are:

Projects - involve completing tasks.

Lifestyle choices - looks at our habits and rituals.

Activities - found in a calendar and are fixed within a time frame.

Note Taking - is about capturing information we may want to take action on at another time.

Spontaneous - is about dealing with the things that come up that we weren't able to prepare for previously.

Understanding our planning style shapes how we approach every new project, schedule our appointments, and really allows us to tap into being organised in a way that doesn't squash your creativity, embraces your uniqueness, and inspires you to take action.

Each different type of planning can be associated with a different set of behaviours.

Project Managers have projects filled with task lists.

Those who prefer Lifestyle Choices are more likely to look at their lists in the form of habits, rituals, or routines.

Activity Schedulers will use a calendar and/or time blocking.

Notetakers will have a more long-form story-based format for the way they want to approach things, but when we look closely, we can still see the sequential steps contained within their paragraphs of text.

Spontaneity seekers tend to want to avoid planning but appreciate systems to solve problems that arise.

The simplest way to ensure you will follow through with your plans is to make sure you are attuned with Your Planner Preferences as you make them.

Each of us has our own unique style when it comes to planning. We can spend years working this out, or we can fast-track the process by using patterns and profiles to get an insight into the way we work.

Project Managers are great at taking a project, seeing the outcome, and breaking it into smaller pieces that are placed on task lists which inspires them to take action.

People with a preference for Lifestyle Choices are more likely to use habits, routines, and/or rituals to help them navigate their way to success. Preferring to create a lifestyle that will help them achieve their goals.

Activity Schedulers love a calendar. They'll turn tasks into appointments. They'll love to see everything in its place on a colour-coded calendar. They'll be heard saying something like "If it's not on the calendar it's not happening."

Unrefined Note Takers may have post-its and notebooks everywhere. They'll be saying something like: "If I don't write that down - I'll forget" The more refined note-takers will still have prolific set of notes storage and they will be using something like the getting organised with GRACE system to keep track of them.

Spontaneous/responsive planners absolutely love the freedom of not being contained by a structure. They tend to leverage other planners to ensure that required tasks are completed on time.

Identifying Your Planning Style empowers you to make choices that are aligned with your personal preferences giving you the greatest chance of making plans that are inspirational for you.

TASK: *Discover your planning preferences using the below quiz.*

The following 10 questions will help you identify your planner preference.

Keep a tally of your answers by the letters next to them in the table found at the end of the quiz.

Q1: What do you find easiest?

P_____Taking a Project and breaking it into small bite-sized tasks

L_____Setting up routines and habits that will achieve your goals

A_____Scheduling Activities and Actions on a Calendar

N_____Discovering and documenting brilliant ideas

S_____Responding to challenges as they crop up

Q2: I feel most organised when I:

P_____Have a clear outcome and list of actions to take

L_____Follow my routines and rituals to create my success

A_____Allocate time to Actions and Activities on a Calendar

N_____Know all my ideas are stored waiting to for action

S_____Am confident in responding to the situation at hand.

Q3: I wish I knew how to better...

P_____Be flexible with how I approach a big project

L_____Allow myself space to break habits and routines and enjoy life more.

A_____Leave space in my calendar for spontaneous activities

N_____Keep track of ideas that I can't implement immediately

S_____Document plans to share with other people

4. Fill in the blank:
To achieve my goals I can't live without my _____:

P_____Task Lists

L_____Habits and rituals

A_____Schedule

N_____Notes

S_____Freedom

Q5: Which of the following is accurate as your mantra

P_____Projects are completed by breaking them into bite size pieces

L_____Habits are the road to success

A_____If it's not in the calendar it's not happening

N_____Discovering and documenting brilliant ideas

S_____Without a deadline nothing would ever get done

Q6. When it comes to planning I most experience:

P_____Overwhelm

L_____Frustration

A_____Guilt

N_____Procrastination

S_____Resistance

Q7. I am most likely to procrastinate when....

P_____I'm unclear of my tasks

L_____I am unable to build a new habit

A_____I haven't allocated my actions a time slot in a calendar

N_____I can't take notes to clear my mind

S_____I don't feel in control of the situation

Q8. I'm most at ease when:
P I'm following a task list
L I'm in flow
A I've got a clear schedule
N I am brainstorming
S I can live in the moment

Q9: It's time to get organised! What do you grab?
P_____My trusty project planner and checklists
L_____A cup of tea - so I can do my mind cleansing ritual.
A_____My Calendar or Scheduling tool
N_____My Bright Ideas Notebook
S_____Organised? What's that?

Q10. You'd rather spend an hour:
P_____Prioritising your Project Tasks
L_____Refining your Routines and Rituals
A_____Colour Coding your Calendar
N_____Brainstorming your Brilliant Ideas
S_____Going with the Flow

Add up your totals for each of the letters and give yourself a percentage overview of your preferences

P____ L____ A____ N_____ S_____
P____ L____ A____ N_____ S_____
Eg.
P - III L - III A - II N - I S__
P - 30% L - 40% A - 20% N - 10% S 0&%

Your score will help you identify your overall preference though I encourage you to keep in mind your individual answers. I'm not going to be so presumptuous to attempt to box you into one style. You are a unique blend of your own combination of preferences. While there are masses of generalisations I could make here, none of them tend to be helpful.

Reflect on your individual answers and allow them to help you when creating plans in the future. There are no better or worse styles, there is simply who you are. Remember the lesson from earlier in the book - the more you can embrace who you truly are and release who you think you need to be, the more room you make for joy and fulfillment in your life.

This is an opportunity for you to close the gap between who you think you should be and who you truly are. Embrace your uniqueness. Leverage your strengths and accept your stretches.

Taking notes or waiting for things to crop up is a form of passive planning and while it will work for some people, if you want to create a home you love, you will probably need to leverage an active form of planning.

Strategic planning requires us to use at least one of the active planning styles at least some of the time. These are Project Management, Lifestyle choices, and/or Activity scheduler.

If you are predominately a spontaneous planner and want to be more proactive ensure you choose one of the other styles to add in or have another person with an active planning preference supporting you. My husband as a spontaneous planner often leverages my love of project management so he can live in the moment, without essential things like paying bills being forgotten.

If your dominant style is notetaker, ensure you choose one of the active three to support you in your proactivity and achieving your goals. It doesn't matter which one, use your percentages to work out which is best for you.

Most household chores can be viewed as activities, routines, or tasks. Your active planner preference will influence which perspective is more motivating and maintainable for you.

For example, making our bed.

This could be viewed as a task contained within the project of tidying our bedroom.

Or it could be viewed as a routine or ritual performed each morning.

Or it could be an activity - marked up on your calendar to be done at 7:15am.

Whether we are using Project management, Lifestyle choices, or Activity scheduling if we want to succeed in managing the many dimensions of creating a home we love we need to value using categories.

Categories may become the names of our projects, how we refer to our rituals, or the number of colour choices we have on our calendars.

How many categories you choose will depend on your preferences for abundance or simplicity.

Choosing your Household Categories

When it comes to managing our home, the main pieces can be sorted in a number of ways. In my home we use the DailyFROG categories - ForMe/Us, Required, Outstanding, & GiveValue.

In her book, Fair Play, Eve Rodsky suggests the following categories: Home, Out, Caregiver, Magic, Wild, and Unicorn Space. However, we choose to break them apart, if we wish to avoid overwhelm, it is essential we utilise categories. Decide if you have category simplicity or category abundance based on your preference.

One of the most common things that household slaves tend to mash together is cleaning, organising, and sorting. When they do this it makes simple tasks become complicated and overwhelming.

Household managers know to look at distinct chores separately. Rather than trying to multi-focus and do 8 things at once, they, at least in their mind, know the different categories in play. When we can distinguish cleaning from tidying we approach it differently. Yes, the temptation to need to tidy first can be exceptionally strong, that old perfection strategy so many of us have creeping in.

Sometimes we have to let that go and be okay to clean around the clutter. Pick things up, wipe underneath them, and put them down. The reason cleaners are so much more time-efficient than many of us is because they are not decluttering or distracted by decisions, they are purely cleaning. They will probably remove obvious trash, but everything else is left for the house owner (or room occupant in a hotel) to manage.

When you want to clean - Clean. When you want to tidy, organise or declutter, do that. Don't try to do or think about all of them at once. This means working out what your categories are and how you distinguish between the various chores in your home. What matters most is that you choose categories and identify the tasks, activities, or lifestyle choices in a way that makes sense to you.

Chances are this is not the first book you've read on productivity, household management, or personal development. It's also highly likely that in the past when you have tried to use other people's systems some have worked wonderfully while others have been a complete flop. Armed with your newfound self-awareness and understanding your preferences you are now far more likely to be able to discern which systems will work for you, and which won't.

Over the next few pages, I will share what works for my husband and I. However, this is not necessarily going to be the best fit for you. In the following section, I will walk you through what you need to consider as you create your own Household Management System.

So, as I shared before, in our home we use FROG as our overarching categories.

I predominately am a Project Manager when it comes to planning style - and so my preference is that we turn most of the chores into Projects containing tasks. There are a few chores that we have as lifestyle choices or routines. It's not black and white. I leverage my preference, while recognising that in some areas lifestyle choices or activity scheduling makes more sense. Especially as Michaels secondary planning preference is lifestyle choices.

While in the past we have had a folder with printed sheets housing information these days we prefer to utilise an Asana board as our "place for everything".

This is a screen shot of our Asana board.

You can access a more detailed screen shot and details of the under-layers in the free book resources at: wisteriaenterprises.com.au/resources

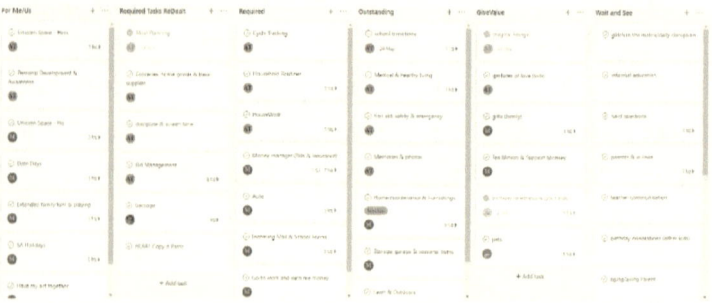

You may be able to see on that image we have 6 main columns and each has almost all the subcategories visible - this makes

it super easy to view all our responsibilities as household managers at a glance.

What I love about Asana is we can have an overview and then we can add sub-categories underneath. With my high preference for category abundance (detailed) this makes me very happy; with my husband's preference for category simplicity, it keeps him sane.

We spent a reasonable amount of time navigating and discussing the various categories and ensuring they were named in a way that made sense for us.

We started with the many lists I've accumulated over the years and adapted them to suit us. I invite you to do the same, either on your own, or with your partner. If you are looking for inspiration my top three recommendations are:

Project Managers:

1. My list - you can download a readable image of the asana example shared above in the online book resources at:

https://www.wisteriaenterprises.com.au/resources

2. Eve Rodsky's Fair Play Card Deck at:

https://www.fairplaylife.com/the-cards

Lifestyle Choices/ Activity Schedulers

3. Flylady Control Journals

http://www.flylady.net/d/getting-started/flying-lessons/control-journal/

TASK: *Identify the categories for you Household Management System*

Making the invisible visible

One of the biggest obstacles when it comes to creating a strategic plan for our household management is that so much of what we do as household managers is invisible. We are so unaware of how much we're doing automatically and how much we are taking care of without thinking about it that we often don't realize what we're doing.

This is also one of the biggest reasons that we have obstacles with bringing our family on board bringing our husbands on board because they're not seeing it. The old adage of a woman's work is only seen when she doesn't do it comes to mind. There's an old story that I've heard many, many times.

A man comes home from work and out the front of the house there are toys strewn everywhere, the front doors open, and the children are running around half naked. He enters the kitchen and discovers food and dishes everywhere. As he looks in the bathroom, he notices there's washing strewn all over the place. In the loungeroom there's toys covering the entire floor. He approaches the bedroom where he finds his wife and he says "Oh my God. What happened? What have you done all day?" And she looks up and very casually replies "All that stuff I usually do every other day. Today. I didn't do it."

What we're doing as household managers gets hidden, it is frequently unseen unless it is undone. Which means a significant part of what we need to do is become very consciously aware of what it is that we're managing. What it is that we need to take care of and how much it is that we're doing. And, even more importantly, we need to approach this filled with compassion. Filled with appreciation, filled with a delight that we live in a world where we get to do this.

What happens all too often when we start listing out everything that we do, and trying to point it all out to our spouses, we feel resentment. We become judgemental asking ourselves (or sometimes them): Why don't they know what we're doing? Why are they so unaware? How are they possibly so oblivious?

And the reason is simple: not everybody thinks the same. Not everybody is aware of these things and when somebody has been taking care of it for so long. The other person is often completely unaware.

While my husband and I have a beautiful relationship, one that we are continuing to grow and evolve. For a long time, the unsaid mentality that he had was "Amy will handle it" At the end of every sentence when he said "it'll work out" - silently behind the scenes, in his unconscious mind, was the add on - because Amy will handle it.

What we need to do is take the time to really look at what is happening, discover what matters to us in our house. What is going to happen next is you start making what happens automatically, what you do silently, the unwritten, unseen todo lists, visible. And we're going to use what is found to fill our categories.

Note: I've gone back to calling them todo lists here because they are filled with resentment, obligation and pressure.

When we can transfer them from being silent todo lists into being strategic plans we give ourselves freedom. Remember strategic plans contain task lists contained within projects, activities that need to happen, and/or lifestyle choices, habits, rituals, routines, using your planning style as an influence on how you do this right now.

When we do this, when we can come from a space of being able to connect with and physically see on a piece of paper everything that needs to be done two things happen.

Firstly, we're able to communicate far more calmly, logically and emotionally with our spouses. So instead of coming through complaints, judgments, or blame we are able to express cleanly and clearly all of the things that are happening behind the scenes.

The budget that gets done, dealing with the kids notes, picking up the toys, all of that automatic invisible stuff starts to become visible. We can't manage the invisible. We can only manage what we can see. Eve Rodsky in her book recommends using physical playing cards to make it even more tangible and real. We opted for digital cards, though I do have printables for a range of tasks. The sheer volume of physical cards (100) was too much for my husband to handle because of his preference for simplicity.

If you want to access my printable cards you'll find them

in the online community resources. Go download it and leverage that if you want the physical experience.

The link again is: wisteriaenterprises.com.au/resources

Keep in mind the different preferences of the people you will be sharing with, both your own levels of overwhelm, and your partner if they are on board (if they are not on board we discuss that more in chapter 9).

Secondly, when we make the invisible visible, we get clear on everything that we're doing. Instead of the silent todo list, and the mental and emotional load of all these things taking up our brain space, all of these things that we're remembering, instead of allowing yourselves to be creative and expressive and passionate and fun filled and sharing joy and delight with the world. You've been filling your minds with tasks and checklists.

When we take them out of our mind and we put them down on paper, remembering what Matthew McConaughey says, we don't write them down to remember, we write them down so we can forget, we can free our mind. No longer will we feel the pressure of having to remember all of these things, because we know it's taken care of, every item in a list that we're going to come back to and review.

With this new found mental freedom we can finally allow ourselves to tap into creativity.

It doesn't matter whether you look at these as projects/tasks, routines, or activities. It doesn't matter whether you add them to lists or schedule them in your calendar, what matters is you make the invisible visible.

TASK: *Fill in the details in your household categories*

Part 3: Movement

Start before you are Ready!

It doesn't matter whether it's cleaning our house, launching a course, or starting a new relationship, the old adage of Ready, Aim, Fire, often gets in our way.

When we think we need to be ready before we take aim, and even more before we take action (and metaphorically Fire) we will get in our way every time.

The pathway to success is to have an idea of the outcome, the target of your action, something to aim towards, and then take action.

We won't ever get ready by wishing and waiting, or reading, but always by taking action.

As much as I am a list lover, and a planning specialist, I know that readiness doesn't come from writing the list, or planning a project, we get ready by taking action, by knowing what we are aiming towards, and shooting the arrow, and getting the feedback.

Our Routines, Expectations, Agenda's, Daily Intentions, and Your Checklists will only be fully created and refined as you take action.

At this point in the book if you haven't been taking action,

I'm really at the end of what I can offer to inspire you. Other than the online community where you will find likeminded people to offer you support and relatability.

There comes a point (and this is it!) where we need to shoot the arrow to discover if we are able to aim well (or not), if we are not strong enough to propel the arrow far enough, if we have a steady hand or if we are going to veer off to the left. The only way to get deeper insights and awareness is through action. We can then identify our gaps, determine what we need most, and go back and learn and apply again until we get success.

Being open to the learning journey, to making mistakes, to getting ready on the journey. The metaphor my mentors often used was to assemble the parachute as you are falling, and frankly in those circumstances I think jumping in when not prepared is unwise. But for something like cleaning our house or decluttering where the consequences are significantly less dramatic we can start, and get ready along the way.

Give yourself permission to develop and refine the Routines, Expectations, Agenda's, Daily Intentions, and Your Checklists that have you feel ready as you go.

Whatever it is you want to achieve, action will be the way to make it happen. We simply must start before we are Ready, because movement, action, is the only way to discover what READY really looks like for us.

Step 7 Creating Sustainable Habits

One of the most common myths about habits is that it takes 21 days to form a habit. Embedding an action so that it becomes automatic can be done in an instant for some things and take years for others.

There are a million things I could talk about with regards to habits (I suspect I've just found the topic of another book to write...) but right now, today, the piece I want to impart is this.

The complexity of what we are aiming to undertake as the habit, the triggers, and so much more influence the length of time it takes to form a habit.

While you are building the habit, let go of how long it will take and focus on what it will take to embed it as a habit instead. Who do you need to be, what will you need to do, to achieve the results you want to have?

One thing that does seem to be consistent in the research is that the smaller the habit is, the easier it is to embed.

Start with Easy Wins

The next few lines will work really well if you read them to the tune "It Started with a Kiss" by Hot Chocolate.

◊ *It started with the cups*
In the drawer in the kitchen
How could I predict
The power of this moment
They stayed still as I moved the drawer
It filled me with such delight
They kept their promise to stay in place
It made me inspired to clean my house
And then, I made the bed
and my motivation arrived (motivation arrived)
I thought that life was always good
I knew how to always stay inspired
Started with the cups
Never thought it would come to this
Started with cups
Never thought it would come to this
I notice every little thing
Like a fork that is out of place
When my control freak issues

Have started to hang around ◇

One of the biggest challenges I have (and I am guessing some of you do too) is motivation to run my business and enjoy my hobbies is largely influenced by how I feel about my home and my desk.

There is a chain reaction from what I see in my home on my way to my office that shapes how I show up (or don't) to give value to others through my online business.

When I walk through my bedroom past an unmade bed, instantly I feel not good enough and like a fraud - it doesn't inspire me to shine my light to the world. Or even to my family.

When I open the drawer to make myself a cuppa and the cups slide and end up in chaos - I feel unworthy and unloved - again not really inspiring going into the world with a strong message that will have some people judge it.

My resilience is very closely linked to how I experience my home (and my relationship with my husband and inner circle but that's a topic for another book).

Recently there was a morning when I went to the cup drawer and the cups stayed put. Hubby had installed a non-slip mat two or three days before and when I saw the cups my whole demeanour changed. I smiled. I was absolutely delighted to see that A) hubby was supporting me and B) something was exactly the way I wanted it to be.

The flow on effect was I made my bed, I folded the plastic shopping bags (being repurposed as rubbish bags), I put away hubbies washing, I got my youngest to put his sheets in the wash, and so much more.

And then, as I was doing these things I felt inspired to

write the parody above and share it with the world. In the hopes I could inspire someone else.

My bed was made and instead of doubt I tapped into my awesomeness. The clothes are away and instead of worrying that I'm not good enough I celebrated the progress.

It was the tiniest shift, with the biggest impact.

Most of the household management experts I've studied have their tiny thing, a ripple action, that they recommend to create a similar chain of events.

Dana from "A Slob Comes Clean" talks about doing the dishes.
Flylady says to put on your shoes.
Konmari suggests folding clothes with joy.

Over the years I've tried (and sometimes failed) with various different trigger mechanisms. My own experience is that enthusiasm will often last a short time and then once I integrate them as 'normal' they lose their impact and I need to search out another to create the same impact.

But, irrespective of the short-term effects, and my need to keep resetting and finding new exciting delightable moments in my home, the impact is there to start. And for many people it is far more long lasting for them than it is for me. I hope, for you, it is the latter, but reassure you if you are more like me, that even the short-term delight is worth leveraging.

It's worth choosing one small thing, an easy win, that you can get done (like making the cups stay still in the drawer, or clearing your bedside table, or wiping down the bathroom sink at night before bed) - anything is worth a try. That one small thing that when you get up will make you smile and inspire you to continue to do things that will create a ripple impact.

Whether we are aware of it or not, what we see, hear, feel, touch, and sense is constantly having an impact on our mood. How we relate to what we notice will determine if our mood goes up or goes down.

Our mood also influences how we relate to things. This is very much a chicken and egg question and one I've never seen resolved consistently as to what comes first our mood or the external trigger.

I get a sense the reason for that boils down to our cognitive functions which sit inside our Myers Briggs Personality types. I'm not going to go into it too in depth here, but very briefly each type has a different sequence in how and where we gather information and what we use to make decisions.

As an ENTP, I know that the world around me has a big impact on my mood. I predominately gather information from the world around me through my intuition, and then I allow my internal logic system to make a choice.

ENTP refers to my Myers Briggs type – you can learn more about them in the online resources at wisteriaenterprises.com.au/resources

Consequently, if the cups move, I sense that my world is rocky, and I conclude I am unsafe.

My husband, an ISFP, makes decisions internally, through his values, and then looks for evidence in the world around him through his senses that supports his choice. The cups moving makes very little difference to his mood.

There are many other patterns in the world of cognitive

functions (16 types in total), these of course can be explored more fully, but for now it's worth considering for yourself how much the world around you impacts your mood.

What destabilises you? What uplifts you? Based on our preferences, the meanings we give things, we have an opportunity to create for ourselves an upward or downward mood spiral as we go through our day.

While I don't always succeed my own goal is to have as many things around me that create an upward spiral of inspiration. I invite you to do the same. Whether it's changing what you see, hear, or touch - working from the outside in. Or changing what you think, feel, and sense working from the inside out. There's no right or wrong in the approach you choose, just what works best for you.

TASK: *Reflect on that moment when you get up that you notice something and the spiral of defeat or demotivation starts?*

What's that one thing you can adjust to start the spiral moving in the direction you desire - one that inspires and uplifts you?

For me, it was the cups not moving. What is it for you?

Build on success

There are different levels of intensity required to Stop, Start, Maintain, or Add to our habits.

Stopping something is the hardest, unless we have a replacement available to meet the needs (most of which are unconscious) chances are while we may be able to stop for a short term, while we are focused on it, when we lose that focus, due to being distracted, overwhelmed, or even relaxed, that old thing will slide straight back into our lives.

Maintaining the status quo of a long-ingrained habit is relatively easy as our neural pathways are accustomed to and built for redoing that action over and over again, however maintaining a habit that hasn't formed the neural connections takes a lot of focus and dedication.

To start something new, and maintain it proves to be somewhat easier than stopping an old habit, but still sits in a space of requiring us to be conscious and focused. Lose focus, and the habit falls away.

The simplest way to improve our habits is to add a new habit to an existing habit.

There are three ways in which we can do this. We can

focus on ensuring we do something before, during, or after the existing habit.

Again, there are increasing degrees of effort for each of these. To aim to do something before an existing habit takes more focus and concentration to remember than to do something during a habit, and the least effort is required when we add a new habit after an old one.

For example, when I wanted to alter my habit of cleaning the kitchen (a task that was familiar) to the mornings instead of the evenings it was simplest for me to tack it onto the kettle. While I was cleaning during the kettle boiling, really it was after I turned the kettle on.

This was an effective shift, until my husband started to be the main tea maker in the house. At which point I rarely boiled the kettle, and so the kitchen went back to being cleaned in a responsive manner rather than a proactive manner.

Adding a habit in before an existing habit or task will require you have a self-initiated cue. Trying to add a habit during an existing habit requires us to disrupt an automatic routine. When we aim to add a new habit after an existing habit the old habit becomes the cue for the new.

According to Charles Duhigg in his book "The power of Habit" - every habit, every action we take automatically has three pieces - the cue, the routine, and the reward.

My mentor who trained me in Meta Dynamics presented me with a similar concept in the form of TOTE. Every habit, every action, has a Trigger, Operation sequence, Test, and Exit.

The trigger, or cue, can be internal or external. We see, hear, think, feel, or sense something. This tells us it is time to run the routine, or operation, associated with that trigger.

The routine or operations is a sequence of steps designed to create a specific result. We don't tend to do things again that don't reward us in some fashion, we test that we got the reward or result we want and then we stop running that routine.

Sometimes we will run the same routine hoping to get the reward even when we know better.

For example, about 10 minutes ago I wanted to boil the kettle. I pressed the button and nothing happened. And while I had a thought that it was probably unplugged and that checking the power point was on and the cord in place occurred to me - I pressed the button twice more before changing my strategy. Completely unconsciously I kept doing what usually gets the desired result, despite consciously being aware that I needed to do something different.

B.F. Skinner in his research on operant conditioning noticed this effect in pigeons. Once we think a certain action will get the result we will continue to do the thing in the hopes of getting the reward, even with evidence to the contrary.

We are all operating mostly unconsciously. Various studies suggest that anywhere between 40% and 95% of our daily actions, thoughts, and feelings are unconscious habits. They occur because they are part of a routine, or operation sequence, in response to a cue.

When I see Mentos, (a peppermint or fruit flavoured

candy – with a crisp shell and a soft- gum like chewable inside) I instantly think of my Grandma. She always had them in her handbag, and I have a very strong association between them and her. If I see Mentos (Cue), I think of my Gran (Operation), I then feel happy (Reward) at the memory. This is all done completely unconsciously.

Because of this breaking a routine, or operation sequence, that has previously given us a reward is complicated. Which is why it is simpler if we add habits after the operation sequence of an existing habit, instead of trying to incorporate an action into the middle of one.

As you try to build your habits, incorporate new routines into your day, be kind and compassionate to yourself, and remember this lesson. Remember that you are a pigeon, who thinks pressing the button after you turn to the right will give you food. As was observed in the experiments by B.F. Skinner.

By focusing on using existing cues (the rewards of our existing habits) we are able to create flow on sequences and longer routines, which will in time become automatic.

Think about your existing habits, which would be valuable to turn the reward into a cue, and add a new habit to the end?

Maybe it's after you turn the kettle on, you wipe down the kitchen bench.

Maybe it's after you drop the kids to school you walk for 10 minutes up and down the street.

It doesn't really matter which small habit you choose to empower yourself with, the purpose of this exercise is to help you realise that by focusing on building on positive habits we can create habit chains, adding one tiny piece, a single link, at a time.

Things with less than 3 steps seem to be easiest. When we start breaking things down, we find that many things have multiple steps.

Going for a walk for example:

Find shoes and put them on.

Find a coat.

Locate my headband (and ensure it is charged) so I can listen to music.

Navigate child logistics so I can leave the house (less so these days, but when my kids were smaller this was a significant piece).

So already we are at 5 steps (some that contain sub-steps) and it is no wonder that we find creating habits hard.

Something like drinking a glass of water when we wake up also contains 3 steps.

1. Locate Clean Glass.
2. Fill with water.
3. Convince ourselves to drink the flavourless item.

So, as we embark on developing new habits, I want you to really ensure you are focusing on a single step. Just the first thing that will then be able to flow on to you following through.

If we use walking as an example, my first step was to find my shoes. If we rewind a step, if I simply always put my shoes (and socks, and headband, and coat) away in the same place every time that step is removed. So, if this was the habit I was wanting to take on as my challenge, my first habit would be to put my shoes away when I take them off. This is what I would bring my attention to most intently. After I take off my shoes, I put them away.

TASK: *Think about your existing habits, which would be valuable to turn the reward into a cue, and add a new habit to the end?*

This section on habits is just one tiny piece – enough for you to get started at home, if you want to continue with empowering yourself to be motivated you may want to check out some of the other resources Wisteria Enterprises has to offer on that focuses on creating a life you love from within. You can find them at: wisteriaenteprises.com.au/resources

The Habit Management Matrix

When we are forming new habits, we often require support to remember and/or ways to measure our progress. Some habits we may simply want a reminder without measuring the success, while others we want to measure success, with or without a reminder.

These two key components, when combined with if a task needs to be scheduled or not, influence habit success and can be combined to create the habit management matrix. The matrix empowers us to know how to best support ourselves in adapting to the new habit.

We monitor progress by using Tracking charts, we support our progress by using Reminders as prompts. We also need to consider if tasks are required to be scheduled or are able to be more fluid.

There is no overall right or wrong with this, it is a personal preference, however, based on our preference (which may vary in different areas) there can be a method that supports us, and a method that holds us back and has old patterns of procrastination, overwhelm, and avoidance kick in.

Tracking vs Reminders

For some people tracking is the best option. They need to see the progress, they appreciate ticking things off. The downside to this can be if there are blanks, some people get demotivated. It all feels too hard and so they stop trying.

For them, reminder lists can be a great thing. Reminders serve as neutral, non-judgemental prompts. Keeping us on track without showing what's not done.

I invite you to take a moment and allow yourself to sense what will best serve you in the areas you are aiming to build momentum through Movement.

For example, in terms of housework I don't want to be reminded of what wasn't done yesterday, I just want a prompt to get me back on track today.

When it comes to tracking my energetic cycles, I hate looking at the half-done charts, they demotivate me and I then don't track at all. Reminders of what is common serves me better.

When it comes to business - I personally prefer to notice what wasn't done, and it spurs me on to do better - in this space tracking and accountability works better for me to feel motivated - long lists of reminders without seeing my progress overwhelm me.

If I was using a reminder for my shoes I would set an alarm at the same time, probably in the evening, each day to check if my shoes are away. In time, I would want to build the habit of putting them away automatically, the reminder and looking for them each night may encourage it.

I trust that helps you see how these can play out in

different areas and how for some things tracking will be needed, for others, reminders will work.

Scheduled vs Looping

The other factor we need to consider is that of recurring tasks. The more you write out your Options lists the more you can notice that when it comes to household management (and raising kids and running a business) so much of what we do happens on a recurring basis.

We have two options when it comes to managing these recurring tasks. Well, two that are functional, there are also many that are dysfunctional such as doing it when we feel like it, ignoring it, &/or wishing, waiting and hoping for someone else to do it.

The two functional options are: Scheduled or Looping.

Depending on your preferences and lifestyle you may prefer one or the other, you may even find in some areas you like one and in others you prefer the other.

Scheduled tasks mean allocating each task in your Options list to a certain day and/or Time, on a weekly, fortnightly, monthly or seasonal basis.

Looping means you have an idea of the frequency of each task and you have a running list that you work through for each time frame but in moments that you can do them rather than them being scheduled to a certain day or time.

For example, my Daily HouseWORK tasks I prefer to do in a looping style. Rotating through each of them as I get time.

Another example is changing the sheets on my bed, while these are done roughly every two weeks they are never scheduled as such.

Others I know prefer to lock in the routine into a time of day. It is entirely your call. The key is for you to be taking action, creating momentum with your movement.

When we combine tracking/reminders and looping/scheduled we get 4 options.

Tracked + Scheduled = Chore Chart/Score Board

Tracked + Looping = Log book

Reminder + Looping = Check lists

Reminder + Scheduled = Alarms/Prompts

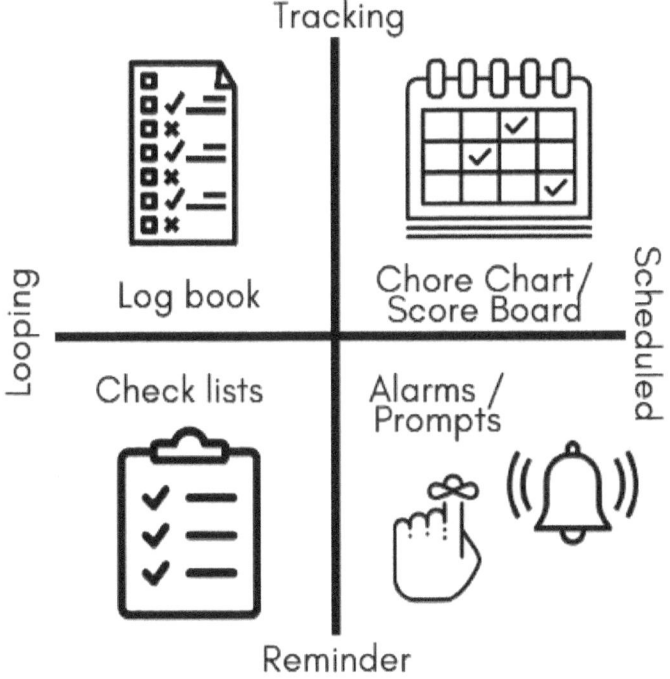

If we look at my household management plans over the last decade or two, I've used all of these at various times.

Right now, my most common practice is to leverage Alarms, with a handful of checklists.

An example of Reminder + Scheduled = Alarms/Prompts

For example, each week I need to access Every Plate and ensure that the menu selected is what we want for the week. This is a recurring task, it doesn't need to be tracked as such, but it does need to be done by a certain time. It is not a habit I have built so I need a reminder.

I have an alarm set in my phone that repeats every week to remind me to log on and check the menus.

An example of Reminder + Looping = Check lists

On the notice board in my kitchen there is a set of lists that remind me of some of my routines. It includes the DailyFROG acronym (which in the past was a reminder + scheduled item, but now I think through it without the reminder as it became an ingrained habit after having done it for 10 years, to the point it's not pretty much unconscious and I run through the 4 dimensions daily automatically). I keep the list in the kitchen as an unconscious reminder. If I feel I need to remember I can look at the list to remind me.

An example of Tracked + Looping = Logbook

Where this is active for me at the moment is teaching my son to drive. We don't have a set day or time when we do lessons, it is done as needed or on availability (looping). We need to track the progress and document the hours. So we use a log book. (Notably it's mandatory for us to do so, but still, it is an example).

Tracked + Scheduled = Chore Chart/Score Board

This is my least favourite, and as I write this, I don't believe I have any active scoreboards. Over the years I have utilised chore charts with the kids to tick off their routines in the morning and various other tasks they were required to do.

I am more likely to use this in my business.

I find them quite demotivation, however some people find them highly inspiring so in the attempt of offering a complete model I have included it.

You get to choose, just as I do, which of these methods of habit management best support you on your journey.

TASK: *Look over your Household Management Plan and make a choice for each item where it sits in the Habit Management Matrix*

Step 8 - Create a Sanctuary

We started this book with me saying that the transformation to your home wouldn't happen overnight. And what we're going to focus on right now is how to continue the journey.

Ideally, we want to make our entire home a sanctuary, everywhere in our home, brings us joy, fulfillment, and lights us up. In the beginning though we need to keep in mind that the transformation still isn't going to happen overnight. You've read the book; hopefully you've taken some actions. I want to remind you again this is a gentle, progressive, compassionate journey. It's probably not something that is going to change overnight, or even within a week or two.

It's worth thinking about how you will create ripples within your home. Over time we're going to expand this out to our entire home. I wholeheartedly believe even if you have children, even if you have a spouse, that this is possible. That you can create ripples. And that you can love your home, even if it is not perfectly spotless all the time.

My home is probably about 75% done in terms of creating

the ripples and moving through different areas, including my children's bedrooms, including my husband's train room, that they are each responsible for maintaining. We've rippled out, over time, but it didn't start with the entire house, that just wasn't possible.

I had to start with a single space, an easy win. Then I could build on my success and leverage the habit management matrix based on my own preferences. I invite you to do the same.

Choose your Starting Point

Over the years I've utilised several different spaces that became my area of retreat, and they were my sanctuary within the chaos of a transitioning home.

I've had craft rooms (and corners). The kitchen has been my sanctuary, at times, my office, and my bedroom. There's really no right or wrong with where you pick as your primary area.

There's no one-size-fits-all way to start the ripples. You'll need to experiment and choose for yourself.

For some people, the front entrance way when you walk into the home is inspirational. As you enter your home, you feel like you can relax, you notice you're walking into your sanctuary. That could be a space to start as well. I imagine there are people out there that choose the bathroom and are able to go in and have a relaxing bath with bubbles and candles as their retreat area.

It doesn't matter where you choose first as your sanctuary, but I want you to think about one space that will create ripples. What's the one space where if it was set up, and you could go there and you could spend some time in that little section of your home you would feel relaxed and be able to rejuvenate?

Don't aim for a whole room to start with, simply aim for a section. I shared the story earlier about how it started with the cups... But over the years it's also been my bedside table. It's been the bathroom sink, there's been a range of things that I've leveraged over the years. Just pick somewhere.

My primary sanctuary is my bedroom. And, while now, it is my entire bedroom, it started with what I see first when I wake up. This is the TV stand. So I started by making sure just that area stayed clean and uncluttered. While our towels live on there, and the TV, we aim to ensure there is nothing else in that space.

My husband may on rare occasions attempt to put his sunglasses there, but they get removed very quickly. His keys and work notes all have a place to go and over time he has embraced that space just needed to stay clear for me and my sanity. He understands, because I have shared with him, if I wake up and look at that space, if it's got stuff on it, instantly I'm resentful. Instantly I'm annoyed. Instantly I feel frustrated. And it's not the way either of us want me to start my day. And so he puts in the effort to help keep it clear.

If you were to pick one space, that is kept clear of clutter, and everything that lives there is organised and in its place, and you could feel the ripple effect of inspiration, where would it be?

Yes, you want your entire house done but your entire house is a lot. Your entire house is not going to change overnight.

Your entire house, even if you've been reading a section a day and implementing, you'll have seen progress, but it's probably not done yet.

And that's okay. It's okay that this is a journey. It really is okay that this takes time. If you've got kids, they're going to undo it just as quickly as you managed to make progress some days. For some people it's their husbands undoing it. For some people, like me, we are the biggest problem to maintaining our home. As much as I would love to blame my husband and kids. If I get down to the truthfulness of it - the biggest problem is me. And that's delightful to me on some level because when the biggest problem is me it's easier to navigate and make changes.

As I've improved the biggest problem has at times shifted to my husband and kids. But the more I take action, the more inspired they are to take action as well and we grow and we learn together.

Your task for this section is to choose a small area, no larger than a metre squared. A desk, bedside table, a shelf drawer, I don't mind what it is. Pick something! Pick something small and achievable. Something that will create ripples.

The goal is that you've got a tiny little piece of your home that is becoming a sanctuary and that is maintained and sustained. And then as that becomes a habit, we can start to create the ripples. I started with the TV stand in the bedroom. Then it was my bedside table. Then it was making the bed than it was the floors in the bedroom. And so I continued through the bedroom and the bedroom became my main sanctuary. And then I can ripple out into the rest of the house. The next area for me will be my office. Like I said, we're about 75% done in my home, and my office is pretty good, but my desk could do with a little bit of care. There's always space and room for growth in this area. I'm not perfect. And I encourage you not to strive for perfection either. Strive for progress. I'm a step ahead. I trust by now you've got something of value from the book, and I didn't need to be perfect and neither do you. We can all do this, we can all grow together. And this is a journey. This is how we create a home we love while also creating a life we love which means not being rigid, not getting caught up in feeling stuck and just making progress one little space of our home at a time.

It's easy to get consumed by wanting to get the WHOLE house, or even an entire room tidy, today I want you to consider thinking about household management in 1m squares or smaller spaces.

We're going to start by finding a 1m square space that is going to be our relaxation spot.

Your relaxed spot could be any of the following:
- a comfy chair,
- your bed,
- your exercise machine,
- your desk, or
- your choice

It is a single space you can go that inspires you, that allows you to feel calm and relaxed, and is the starting point of creating a whole home sanctuary.

If you want to create the home you love, we need to make the time to start (you may not complete in the first attempt, just start) and declutter, then clean. Initially focus on just a small space. Then keep going one small space at a time.

TASK: *Choose your Sanctuary starting point. Clear it, clean it, and set yourself up with one of the habit management tools to maintain it.*

Three styles of decluttering.

Way back in chapter three, we explored what the experts say about the philosophy of decluttering. And we explored the clutter threshold and the container concept, and we didn't really get into the finer details of "How" to declutter. And so now it is time to take those philosophies to take those concepts and start putting them into action.

I'd love to share with you three different strategies for decluttering.

1. No Mess Method
   Pull it out and get it done
2. Small area
3. Large area

I learned the No Mess Method from Dana from "A Slob Comes Clean" in her book "Decluttering at the Speed of Life." One of the most common issues people face when decluttering or attempting to organise their home is that they create more mess as they go, and there becomes a significant impact on their life.

It becomes overwhelming and frustrating. The pull it out methods take time and energy and don't allow room for interruptions. For many of us that time and energy is a luxury we just don't have. Which is why I most often recommend the No mess method.

his method is great if you:
- feel you may be interrupted,
- only have a limited time available,
- are not sure how long your energy will hold out,
- are easily distracted and/or
- get bored quickly.

Pick an area you want to declutter. I invite you to take a before photo, more to remind yourself of the progress. And then instead of pulling everything out, you're going to just take a minute or two and remove one item at a time as you can see them. At the end you'll have made progress (it won't be perfect) and you'll have no mess.

Look at the area and start to remove any obvious trash.

Once the trash is removed assess if there are some no brainer, no choice needed, they are so obvious, donations - go place them in your donatable donations box.

Look again, is there something there that doesn't belong in this space - pick it up, and anything else that belongs in the same area it does gather what you can comfortably hold.

Take the items to the other area straight away. While the aim is not to get distracted, the benefit of this method is even if we do, the area being worked on is no worse than it was before, so progress is still made with no mess to clean up.

When you remember, go back to that area and start to apply the container concept. If it doesn't fit in the container - you need to make choices. We can only keep what fits comfortably in our containers.

The second method that I'm going to share is the flip to the no mess method. It is the pull everything out and work through sorting and then putting things back.

There are two conflicting philosophies for this method - and both have a place.

Flylady says don't ever pull out more than you can put back in a session. Whereas Konmari says pull out everything like they do on the TV shows like "Life on the lawn."

This means this approach can be done on a small or large scale. There are benefits and disadvantages to each.

If we pull out everything we can easily see everything. This can be great to easily survey and make choices based on the A/B matrix, however, it can also increase overwhelm and anxiety.

One way to decide between whether you utilise the no mess method or whether you utilize a pull-out everything method big or small is to explore your tolerance levels for chaos. This is based on your ability to get things done while considering your life and family circumstances.

Dana from "A Slob comes Clean" named her book "Decluttering at the Speed of Life" and I think these are such wise words, and a great way of allowing us to consider the speed and intensity we want to apply to the journey.

In 2016 I was able to carve out three weeks of my life and just dove in and did the entire house following the Konmari - pull it all out approach. I didn't need to cook, clean, or attend to the children as my husband was home and he took care of everything. I was able to dedicate my entire focus to just making choices and sorting our home. It got quick results but was exceptionally intensive. If you have the time and you can dedicate the time it will get you the results quickly and it will get it done. And it was wonderful, but each year I do a Spring Reboot of my home, and I have never chosen to do it that way again. Much preferring to do a combination of the no mess method and pulling out small areas that I can complete in an hour or two.

How you choose to approach rebooting your home is entirely up to you. Look at your own preferences, capacity and commitments and make a choice.

Are you going to do the no mass method? Are you going to do the pull it out on a small area or are you going to do the pull it all out on a large area?

Whichever method you choose, the way we SORT is the same.

There are four categories that we can use. When it comes to paperwork, we've got the decide with EASE method, and these are very similar, with a slight tweak in language. Again, it's keeping the choices simple. SORT, of course, is an acronym.

S is for Stays. - It belongs in the space you are organising.

O is for Other space in your home. It's something you want to keep, but it's not something that belongs in this space.

R is for Rehome. This is something that is still useful, is still functional, could be loved by somebody else, but no longer brings joy or productivity to you. These are donations by any other name.

T is for Trash. And that's self-explanatory, it's rubbish. It's broken, it doesn't work. It's something that you don't think you can rehome, if its trash get rid of it.

Whichever method we choose we need to stay focused. Distractibility is one of the biggest problems you will need to overcome. The no mess method is great for people who are highly distractible because if you get distracted, you've made no mess and it doesn't matter so much. If you're pulling everything out, you're going to need to have a higher level of focus available to you. The level of focus you can access will determine how much stuff is reasonable for you to pull out. If you have a very short attention span, utilise the no mess method. If you have a moderate attention span and ability to maintain focus you could probably go with a small to mid-range area. To use the pull everything out method and do it all in one large hit, you will need a substantial level of focus and time available.

TASK: *Assess your distractibility levels by starting with the No Mess method and a small area (a single drawer) with the pull it out method. Make a choice which works best for you.*

To sell or not to sell. That is the question.

Over the years, every decluttering expert that I have watched and every household management expert that I have paid any attention to, has suggested to donate and just let go of the stuff. I can't think of anybody (and if you know someone, I'm open to it) who is striving to create the home they love that is trying to sell stuff to recoup costs for whatever it is.

We need to recognise the money is spent.

While I understand about financial pressures and not knowing how you're going to pay the bills, I have never got any joy from selling items on Gumtree or Facebook marketplace. We have been a single income family with four children, navigating and aiming to grow, and build extensions, and all of the usual living expenses. I've lived there, knowing that we've had massive debt, feeling like we were going backwards financially. Many, many years ago, I calculated how much we were spending, and we were spending 132% of my husband's income. It wasn't just that we felt like we were going backwards, we literally were going backwards financially. And still, it always cost far too much in time and energy than to ever make it worth the financial reward.

What I found is that the more I embrace donating, the more I give away what's not being utilized, what's not being loved in my house, the more abundance seems to come back to me. I love freecycle and the free groups on Facebook because I was able to generously give and almost always I was able to generously receive what we needed as well.

When we let go of the misconception that we need to recoup the costs we create space for joy and fulfillment in our lives. This goes back to asking ourselves: are they reasons or excuses? Are you holding on to this thing in the hope of selling it so that you can navigate past your excuse? "I spent so much money on it. I need to get the money back."

This is my philosophy around this, and you choose your philosophy. I've said the whole way throughout this book, we are unique. We have our own preferences. There is no one size fits all. I'm not aiming to tell you what to do. In this chapter. I'm simply sharing my own experience.

For me, selling and trying to sell and listing things on marketplace generally costs way more time and energy than it is ever worth. While sometimes I will put things up for low prices it is not from a place of recouping the costs but more leveraging what I know of marketing. I find it's really fascinating to explore the psychology of people's buying strategies. Sometimes free stuff is not picked up, but if you put a two or $3 price tag on it, they're grabbed fairly quickly. And so you want to be able to market and get rid of this stuff if you can't just donate it.

Through COVID lockdowns, all of our local donation

centers got locked down and closed their doors because they were getting too many donations. Many people were going through their house and removing excess. Some items I wanted to pass on. I didn't want to just throw them out.

Now at a pinch and I've seen other experts recommend this too, if you can't donate it, if you can't give it away, if you can't sell it, then it's okay to throw it out. I will admit that I struggle with that concept a little bit, but in terms of the costs to our time and our energy, compared to how much walking past the boxes in the hallway weighs down on me emotionally, I can see they have a point.

These items get added to our silent todo list, they provide a physical reminder that I need to do something. Waiting to list or donate them becomes too much. And so there are things that I have just sent to the tip because it was too hard to sell. It was too hard to rehome them and I needed them out of my space, and to keep the promise that I made to myself. This isn't something that I recommend as an ongoing strategy.

The promise that I make to myself is that moving forward I will make better decisions when I'm purchasing things. I aim to make better decisions when I am sorting through things. The decisions that we made in the past can't continue to weigh us down. Well they can, but ideally we move forward from them. The decisions we made in the past need to be released and we get to make new decisions now. If we can sell items, if we can give things away, if we can donate them by all means do that. But if you can't, your mental health is on the line. If it's taking you too much time and energy to facilitate that, please do what you need to do to create the home you love. And if that means that quality things end up in the tip, that is the consequence that happens, and moving forward we make better decisions. Sometimes we just need to acknowledge that we've made a mistake to move forward from it.

Sometimes we need to do things that are not necessarily ideal, but it's how we move forward. All of this is about you making progress and you creating a home you love, creating a life you love, and ultimately expanding out, even beyond that creating the world we love, that's not filled with rubbish in tips. However, do whatever you need to do to get whatever it is you need right now. And serve yourself because you deserve the space. You deserve it, the emotional freedom. You deserve to be able to release yourself from what's not serving and doesn't bring you joy. If it's not being used by you, I don't care if it's useful, if it's not being used by you, and you don't have space for it, whether that's physical, mental or emotional space, allow yourself to release it any way you can.

TASK: *Find something to release. Allow yourself space to say goodbye to something that's no longer serving. Maybe you'll sell it, maybe you'll donate it. Maybe you'll just pick it up and put it in the bin, and allow yourself to have the peace and freedom that you are worth.*

Step 9 Getting your family on board

I'm going to start this by saying that there is another entire book I could write on this subject and at some point, I may, for now though, I hope these tips are enough to get you started.

Let's start by narrowing down the biggest obstacle that gets in the way of people bringing on board their families. And that is communicating expectations from a place of criticism, contempt, judgement, and blame. This creates a whole bunch of uninspiring ways of telling our family what we want from them.

And frankly, I've been there, I've done all of them! Every single possible one that you could potentially come up with, I've done it. I have been a micromanager, a bitch, I have pushed to the extreme. My husband, who somehow, has remained patient through almost all of my learning and growth, and navigating through things like postnatal depression, many existential crises, not knowing who I am or who I want to be. And his ability to see the good in me through all of that has been amazing. He is also flawed and human as well. And I can absolutely complain about him.

However, what I want you to take away from this is the power in seeing the good in those around us. Please don't read into my husband's patience that you have no hope with your own husband. I promise you everything you are thinking about your partner, I have thought too at some point about one of my live-in partners, and most likely my husband. Short of physical abuse and significant emotional manipulation I believe that there is potential to transform the way in which you engage with your family.

(There is also hope with abuse cases, but it is well beyond the scope of this book - if you are in an abusive situation please seek appropriate help).

Apply the TODAY Principles to your family

This book started with focusing on TADA lists for ourselves. Now it's time for you to start creating TADA lists for your family. Focusing on the Things Already Done & Accomplished by them. And this could be a stretch, this could be a really huge stretch. But if we start with taking care of TODAY principles and bring them to the family dynamics. We create space for them to step up. We create space for them to take responsibility. We find a way that they can also join in on this journey. When we stop judging, blaming, criticising, condemning, and expecting, we get different results.

It's really important that we apply the principles of taking care of TODAY, not only to ourselves but also to our family. When we stop looking at what's not done by them and start looking at what is bringing in the principles of the Tada list, then we see them differently. And as our attitude shifts from a place of contempt, criticism, judging, and blaming, to a place of gratitude, hope, inspiration, and passion. We create a different environment in which they step up and start to take responsibility. They start to take ownership. They want to help out around the house because they no longer feel like they have to.

When we bring in the principles of autonomy, competence, and time; we change the game. When we stop giving them a list of essential things laden with obligation, pressure, or stress; and instead give them options they are more likely to be motivated and inspired. When we stop telling them what they have to do and we start giving them choices, they're more likely to help. When we stop telling them what they're doing wrong and invite them to develop their competency, they're more inspired to take the initiative.

I trust you get the point here. The principle of this is to take everything you've learned on how to bring compassion to yourself, inspire and motivate yourself and start applying it to the people around you. And that's going to mean letting go of resentment. It's going to mean letting go of blame. It's also going to mean letting go of expectations. And when you can let go of the expectation that the people in the house will live up to who you think they should be and you start loving them for who they truly are, this is where the game really changes.

Creating space for them to step up and take responsibility requires you to shift your perspective about who they are. It requires you to let go of any of the judgments. You know how to do this, go back to the beliefs exercise in chapter

Ask yourself what you believe about your husband. Who is your husband? When you look at your husband, are you doing it through the eyes of criticism, contempt, and judgment or are you doing it through the eyes of care, compassion, and connection?

When you look at your kids, are you somehow taking that role of household slave that you hated so much, and placing it onto them?

It's so important that we let them become the authority in their life. We can start by allowing them to become the master of their own room.

We can then add to this by giving children zones they are responsible for in the house. Give each child a zone in collaboration with them. Don't just give it to them. Have a conversation. Let them choose what they want to take responsibility for. And I get it, at this point resistance may bubble up. Even just then in my own head as I'm speaking this out, which will then get translated into text in my own mind there was a moment where I went: "Yeah, but if I only let them take responsibility for what they want, nothing will get done". We've got to let go of that bullshit belief. Yes, there's a whole bunch of things in the home that nobody wants to do. But if we nag, criticise, condemn and complain, we know that strategy doesn't work.

What works is to share how we feel about it. What works is to genuinely ask for help with no expectations. What works is to empower the people around us to have autonomy, to have a list of options, these are the options, and when we let go of everything as being essential. If we let go of the "how" it's done. And start focusing on "what" needs to be done. We create an environment that promotes Autonomy and leverages existing competencies.

For example, cooking dinner. We need food. That's a basic life essential. Someone needs to cook dinner, but do we need a three-course meal cooked with whatever it is that we're thinking about every night? Probably not. Can your 12-year-old cook two-minute noodles and add in a packet of frozen peas?

Of course, it's not the most nutritious meal. But that's what they're competent at. Start with their competency, ensuring they've got autonomy. And then we can start building their competencies. And yes, it takes time. Yes, it's faster to do it yourself. But you hate doing it yourself. And that's why you're so filled with resentment. This is the opportunity for you to step back. And take what you've learned in understanding how to inspire yourself and share it with your family.

TASK: *Apply the principles of taking care of TODAY to your family.*

Be Inspirational - take care of yourself first.

If you're not feeling inspired yet, go back and reread the book. Because we cannot inspire someone else, if we are not feeling inspired ourselves. No-one can motivate someone else. Especially if they are not stepping up and taking responsibility and being motivated themselves. We cannot ask of others what we do not demonstrate to them. If someone shows up with resentment, criticism, or contempt, that's what they'll get back. When we come with hope, inspiration and recognition that everybody is entitled to have a choice, that's what we'll get back instead.

We can express things as complaints. Or we can express them as a needs and share our feelings. For example, we can say: I hate cooking dinner. A complaint. Not overly inspirational. Or we can say "Somebody needs to cook dinner tonight. I'm feeling really tired." While the shift won't happen overnight, in time you will start to hear back "I'll take care of that".

My kids cook dinner. My husband cooks dinner. And it's

never been because I've got better at nagging, complaining, bitching, nor because I've got better at 'making' them do it. What I've got better at is being vulnerable, expressing my needs cleanly, and sharing my emotional experiences. And lowering my expectation that the world around me is required to meet them. My entitlement often got in the way of clean expression of a need.

It's important that while we can ask others to help us we also remember that no one is obligated to meet our needs. (*** Side note here - if we are parents of younger children we are responsible for meeting their needs - as adults no one is entitled to make requests of another person to do something for them - we may ask for them not to do something - more on this later in the chapter). Certainly not our children, and not even our spouse.

We may even ask them to do things for us, without expectation, without an entitlement mentality. Recognising that they have a choice as to whether they meet our needs or not. When we come from a place of inspiration, love, reciprocity, and interdependence they often will.

One of my needs is that the clothes in the bedroom drawers are folded neatly. If they're not folded neatly, I feel anxious. But that's my need and it is not my husband's responsibility to meet it. And so I take the time to fold and put away the washing so I don't feel anxious. I am responsible for my feelings. My husband cares for my feelings and does his best not to unfold the clothes in the drawers out of respect for me and a desire to fulfill my needs. But I choose to meet the need for tidy clothes myself. I could also choose to do some healing work and resolve why the messy clothes trigger me so much, but I like the outcome, so I've never dug deeper in that area. I have in other areas.

I need time out and I meet that need for myself and that means that I have to surrender to there being two minute noodles with peas cooked for dinner. Normally green beans in our house. But if I want time for myself, I need to be willing to give up perfectionism in myself and those around me. I need to allow space for autonomy. We need to allow space for creativity in how the outcome is achieved. While expressing what we need.

TASK: *Practice the art of expressing your needs instead of complaints.*

This is a long term game. This is something you're going to have to play with, you will need to develop competency, lean into making it feel autonomous, and allow time for it to unfold. But if you want your family to take responsibility, you want your family to take ownership. If you want your family to take over some of the tasks in the day-to-day running of the house, you're going to have to give up unrealistic expectations and you're going to have to be patient enough for tasks to be done badly to start with. Because the moment we criticise, judge, give feedback through contempt, we destroy autonomy, and we crush the belief that they had in their competency. When those two things are gone, they're not going to want to give you the time to do what you're asking them to do.

This can leave us feeling disheartened and annoyed. When our family doesn't meet our needs, and we don't know how to meet our own needs it can be very lonely which is why it is so key that we find a community for support.

Take the pressure off you and your family, by finding a community

We all need to surround ourselves with people who are responsive to our feelings who are competent and capable and willing to meet our needs as we learn how to do this for ourselves.

When choosing a community, you want to take into consideration who is capable and willing to meet your needs.

Who can help soothe your anxiety? Remind you that you are not alone in this wild and crazy journey called life? Who wants to inspire you and encourage you?

You get to choose what it is that you need from a community. I personally need validation and I hang out with people that validate me.

I work best with company and so I hang out with people with similar projects to me, such as coaches, authors, course creators, and changemakers; the creatives and the pioneers.

I like to receive gratitude when I share my wisdom and critical thinking, so my business community is filled with people who express appreciation when I give them my gifts. What do you need from a community? Who are you looking for?

What are your deficits? What are your gaps? What are the needs you can't meet for yourself, yet? And where can you find people that are willing to give that?

My clients need direction and clarity. My clients need someone that can take a bigger goal and break it down into easy-to-manage steps. That's what they come to me for. My daughter comes to me for cuddles. Attention and physical affection are her most expressed needs. I am willing and able to meet that for her.

My second son at the moment needs driving lessons. That's what he comes to me for. My oldest son needs a little bit of guidance and a reminder that he's capable of saving up for a house.

What do you need reminding of and who in your world can give that to you?

The difference between being needy, and sharing our needs, lies in reciprocity. There is always something we can give to others. My kid's reciprocity is more wonky - they take more than they give some days and that is okay, for kids.

My clients give me money, validation and gratitude and I give them what they need. My accountability buddies: I give to them what they need, and they give back what I need.

Neediness occurs when we believe the misconception we have nothing to bring. There is always something we can give to others. Be as willing to give as you are to take. Tap back into the chapter on strengths if you need to remind yourself what you can and do give on a regular basis.

Becoming willing to meet your own needs, to ask for them, and to meet those of others, is how we create deep meaningful relationships and inspire others to enjoy being on this journey of life together.

I still seek to have my need for validation met by others. But my need for soothing, (which I ignored for a long time), I can now pretty much do for myself most of the time. This means when I go to someone seeking validation, I also have the capacity to meet some of their needs.

Previously my capacity was far lower because I hadn't recognised my anxiety and the need for soothing. This made me needy.

We aren't aiming to become reliant. We're not looking for other people to meet all our needs for us. Sometimes we're looking for the person to teach us how to meet our needs for ourselves.

A healthy community functions on three levels: Aligned, Aspirational, and Leveraged qualities and capacities.

Aligned - What do you want this the same between you and the people in the community?

Aspirational - What are you wanting to do or are you aspiring to become?

Is it more self-compassionate? Is it more focused? Is that more outgoing? Look for the people that are doing and being who you want to become so that they can encourage you to be able to do that for yourself.

And then what are the things that you don't want to learn - that you just want to leverage from people around you?

Be aware that whatever you're leveraging from someone else - keeps you Reliant.

Any of your inner world needs, anything related to your mental well-being, you won't want to let yourself down. These are ideally aspirational values, though may start out as being leveraged.

Validation is something I leverage in people around me all the time, but I am also aware that I have to learn to do it myself. Self-Compassion was something I used to leverage from people but I've learned to do it for myself. Self-soothing when I'm anxious. I've learned to do it for myself at least most of the time. These are all competencies. These are all skills. And they're all worth putting the time, energy, and effort into learning because you deserve to be self-reliant when it comes to meeting your inner world needs. When it comes to things like cooking dinner, cleaning the toilet, building a business, those external world things by all means leverage them. Find someone that has that as their superpower and leverage it.

When it comes to you and your mental health, do what it takes to become self-reliant and accept the gifts from others. There is a difference between reliance, independence, and interdependence. And a community is built on interdependence. You bring your gifts, I bring my gifts, and together we are stronger for it.

TASK: *Find a community support system for your ongoing journey.*

Part 4: Experiences

And here we are, hopefully now friends, on the last page. Maybe you skipped here to see how it ends...

Maybe you hate endings and anticipate the feeling of emptiness that sets in at the end of a TV series you've just binged watched on Netflix..

Either way, you choose, you choose how this ends. You choose if this is the end, or indeed if it is the beginning. While there will be no more chapters in this book, there are plenty more to read, plenty of other books, you get to choose your Experiences.

You get to combine your Heart, the Operations you choose, and the Movement you make, these things combined will create your experiences.

It may be the end of this book, but if you want to continue our relationship there are many options available to you.

Courses, content, communities, and so much more all available to you if you choose to continue this journey.

So, while, for now, this is the end of this book, there are always opportunities for new beginnings.

About Wisteria Enterprises

Our core philosophy is based on the Wisteria plant – which climbs to it's highest potential using the available resources.

While we value sharing resources, we know that true transformation occurs, allowing us to create a life we love, when we empower our clients to access their resourcefulness.

Wisteria Enterprises provides a range of services including Online Communities, Group Mentoring, VIP 1:1 Coaching, downloads, books, and online courses all of which focus on personal growth at home, in business, and from within.

Topics explored focus on Creating a Life we Love, at home, in business, and from within.

Other courses/books by Wisteria Enterprises focused on At Home include:

Living with Flo - leveraging cyclical energy to increase productivity

Design your success – set goals that you are willing to do what it takes to achieve

Website: www.wisteriaenterprises.com.au

Acronym and Model List

3 steps to a Habit - Cue, Routine, Reward

4 Versions of Selves

5 Key relationships - past, passions, possessions, people & perceptions

A/B Choice System

ACT - Autonomy, Competence, Time

Big Fish, Little Fish, Cardboard box

Clutter Threshold

Clutterbugs

Community functional levels

Aligned, Aspirational, Leveraged

Container Concept

DailyFROG - ForMe, Required, Outstanding, & GiveValue.

Disney Strategy

EASE - Execute, Allocate, Store, Erase

FOG - Frustrated, Overwhelmed, and Guilt-ridden.

FROG - Fulfilled, Resilient, Organised, & Gratified.

GIVENS - Global, Identity, Values, Rules, Experiential, Neurological wiring & Situational.

GRACE - Gather Reflect, A place/list for everything, Come Back, & Engage

Habit Management Matrix

HEART - Hope, Energy, Archetypes, Relationships, Thinking

HOME - Heart, Operations, Movement, Experiences

Hope - Passive vs Active

Input types

J.U.S.T.I.F.Y - Joy, Usefulness, Space, Time, Identity, Finances, Your Preferences

No mess method

PLANS - Projects, Lifestyle choices, Activities, Notes, Spontaneous

Purpose Statement Questions

READY - Routines, Expectations, Agendas, Daily Intentions, and Your Checklists.

Ripple Habits/Actions

SORT - Stays, OtherSpace, ReHome, Trash

Survival Archetypes

TADA - Things Already Done & Accomplished

Task Title Transformation

TOTE - Trigger, Operation, Test, Exit

Task Summary

PHASE 1: HEART

Step 1 Taking Care of TODAY

- Plan and take action on your DailyFROG,
- Create your options list.
- Celebrate your TADA's each and every day.

Step 2 Getting to the HEART of the matter

- Use active Hope and move.
- Start to explore which archetypes come out in different areas of your life.
- Identify an action that would prove a belief that's holding you back to be untrue and go do it.

Step 3 Leverage what the Experts say

- Pay attention to which question lights you up more when it comes to decluttering - is it asking if something brings you joy or does it fit in the space?
- Identify your Clutterbug preferences by looking at an area in your house that you use often and is working well for you.
- Put together your own philosophies on decluttering, organising and maintaining your home - using all 3 Disney Perspectives - Dreamer, Analyst, and Critic.

PHASE 2: OPERATIONS

Step 4 Make decisions in advance

- Identify the people in your life you can call on when you need to be supported, challenged, or encouraged.

- Practice identifying how you are Justify-ing with easy things.

- Decide what is it you want from your house and create a Purpose Statement

Step 5 Approach your plans with Ease and Grace

- Assess if the decisions with EASE formula works for you. Rename the categories if it helps you connect with it more. Practice making choices using the key questions.

- Identify your needs, categories, and platform and get clear on the place for all your lists.

- Decide when you will next look at your lists and engage with them.

Step 6 Strategic Planning

- Discover your Planning Preference using the Quiz
- Identify the categories for your Household Management System
- Fill in the details in your household categories.

PHASE 3: MOVEMENT
Step 7 Create Sustainable Habits
- Identify one thing you can use to inspire moving in the direction you desire.

- Think about your existing habits, which would be valuable to add a new habit to the end?

- Look over your Household Management Plan and make a choice for each item where it sits in the Habit Management Matrix

Step 8 Create a Sanctuary
- Choose your Sanctuary starting point. Clear it, clean it, and set yourself up with one of the habit management tools to maintain it.

- Assess your distractibility levels by starting with the No Mess method and a small area (a single drawer) with the pull-it-out method. Make a choice on which works best for you.

- Find something to release. Allow yourself space to say goodbye to something that's no longer serving. Maybe you'll sell it, maybe you'll donate it. Maybe you'll just pick it up and put it in the bin, and allow yourself to have the peace and freedom that you are worth.

Step 9 Getting your family on board
- Apply the principles of taking care of TODAY to you family.

- Practice the art of expressing your needs instead of complaints.

- Find a community support system for your ongoing journey.

References

Amy Wrzesniewski
- Jobs, Careers, and Callings: People's Relations to Their Work

Brian Tracy
- Eat that Frog

Caroline Myss
- Sacred Contracts

Cassandra Aarson
- ClutterBug Profile
- clutterbug.me

Charles Duhigg
- The Power of Habit

Dana White
- A Slob comes Clean
- Decluttering at the Speed of Life
- Container concept video:
www.youtube.com/watch?v=_24PoIZSmVs "

David Allen
- Getting Things Done

Dawn Madsen
- "The Minimal Mom",

Eve Rodsky
- Fair Play (Book) - www.fairplaylife.com/the-cards

Flylady
- www.flylady.net/d/getting-started/flying-lessons/control-journal/

KonMari- Marie Kondo
- The Life-Changing Magic of Tidying Up

Matthew McConoughey
- Greenlights

Self Determination Theory - Edward Deci and Richard Ryan
- https://selfdeterminationtheory.org/the-theory/

Sharon Pearson
- Disruptive Leadership

About Amy Taylor

Amy is a multipassionista on a mission to inspire more creativity, joy, and passion in the world.

As a Mum to four kids, married to a shift-working train-obsessed husband she always wanted a business she could fit in between school picks and drop-offs. She now owns 1 cat, but for a long time owned 7. She has also owned and cared for many chickens (for as long as the foxes allow).

As an expert in patterns, profiles, and preferences, she offers a unique perspective to strategic planning, your way.

Since 2015 she has spent masses of time immersed in studying, applying, and sharing personal development experiences. Launching Wisteria Enterprises at the same time.

She has worked as a paid mentor for Australasia's largest coaching school and has mentored hundreds of budding coaches and business owners.

She is a lover of logic and has created a number of acronyms and models in her time. She enjoys jigsaw puzzles, has performed stand-up comedy in front of a live paying audience and can solve the Rubiks cube in under 2 minutes.